AF326542

LONELY GRADUATION:

The Journey After the Milestone

by **Christopher S. Dennis, PhD**

Lonely Graduation: The Journey After the Milestone

For permissions, inquiries, and speaking engagements, contact: The Campus Culture Group
www.campusculturegroup.com
cdennis@campusculturegroup.com

ISBN: 9780997794250 First Edition

Contents

PART I

INTRODUCTION:
THE MOMENT AFTER
THE MOMENT

My Story:
The Night of My Graduation

Welcome to Lonely Graduation.

This concept, this mindset, began to take intellectual shape sometime between 2012 and 2020, but its roots were seeded even further back. It started with a single moment: the night of my undergraduate graduation in the spring of 2005.

That day, I should have felt on top of the world. My mother had traveled to Minnesota, and my sister had flown in from California; I was excited. I had done it—crossed the finish line, just as every brochure, scholarship program, and piece of media had promised those who enrolled in and/or worked hard through college. I was supposed to feel elation, fulfillment, and pride. And yet, something felt off.

That night, my sister and I drove somewhere that I can't even remember. I do remember what happened in the car. We had an emotional conversation, not an argument, but rather a moment of raw, unfiltered truth. I wanted to be celebrated and feel seen in this moment of achievement, but my sister reminded me that while I had been off building my future, life didn't pause for everyone else. She had carried her own struggles, navigated her own path. She helped me realize that my moment wasn't just mine; it occurred as realities of those who cared about me and yet had their own paths to navigate.

And that's when I realized a raw truth: my graduation was lonely.

Not because I was physically alone since there was plenty of love surrounding me, but because at the peak of my achievement, I faced a sobering question: What now? The climb had been challenging, but no one had prepared me for the silence at the summit. No one had told me that achieving a life milestone often means starting over. I had a job lined up. In fact, I had interviewed for it the morning of my graduation. I knew what was next in a practical sense, but emotionally, I was lost. Lonely Graduation began there.

Fast forward 20 years to 2025. It's May, it's a Sunday, and I'm back on the graduation stage—this time for my Ph.D. I completed a six-year journey to earn my Doctorate in Education for Social Justice from the University of San Diego. The same cast of characters are here to celebrate me. On this day, my sister and both of my parents are here, and we're joined by my wife and three of my five children. My sons are present, and my two daughters are watching online from Houston and Nashville. I mean, my sister did teach me how to read as a kid, so she wouldn't miss this! While the conversation I had the night of my undergraduate graduation was emotional, it led to an awareness of my impact beyond myself. I arrived at my doctoral graduation fully aware of what challenges, stressors, tensions, and expectations awaited me. I knew that if there was a particular way I wanted to be supported, taken care of, or understood, I needed to set those expectations for myself and hold no one else accountable for what I needed in my moment.

About a month before my doctoral commencement ceremony, I confided to my therapist that I was considering skipping it. He responded in a way that, for me, was especially important to hear from one Black man to another:

"Somebody needs to see you cross that stage."

It snapped me back into reality. My sense of duty to others helped me make my decision. I couldn't accept preventing someone else from reaching their potential if my presence crossing the stage could be a motivator. That's wild!

To an extent, I was battling an aspect of internalized oppression that resulted in a dimming of my own light. I played into the safe passage of humility that has at times required professional survival, of measuring and calculating emotion. However, it turned out that the person who needed to see me cross that stage was me.

Have you been there? Are you there now? Anyway, I digress.

Therapy was also a healthy resource I used to prepare for this next stage of life as a professional and scholar. I didn't engage in therapy because I was in crisis, but because I needed tools for the journey ahead and a space to put my bags down before I ventured further. Using therapy as a resource with goals and intention in mind is something that I learned to add to my toolkit through life's transitions, through these major stages or graduations of life.

But back to my doctoral graduation.

After crossing the stage and being hooded, I waited for my family to meet up with me after the ceremony. Once we all gathered, I took off my hat, robe, and hood and began placing an item on each of my family members— first on my mother, then on my father, and then on my sons. I wanted them to feel what I was feeling in that robe with those adornments. I know they probably couldn't fully grasp the magnitude of what it felt like to carry the six-year journey I traveled, but they could at least feel the weight of the garments on that day and in that moment. I hope that if they needed to, they could begin to reverse-engineer what they witnessed during those six years while I was "busy," with an understanding of what I was working toward.

Many years after my undergraduate experience, I realized that I didn't have to sit in the loneliness of graduation. I could embrace the significance of the moment and carve out personally meaningful parts of it to share with others on my day.

Lonely Graduation is about the moment after the milestone. This book delves into how you can prepare for that moment and spend your time embracing the energy that comes from within because you have achieved something important, something significant. This book gives you language to match the feelings you hold and that have held you as you reached your goal.

Why This Concept Matters

We don't talk enough about what happens after we reach our major goals. The world celebrates the milestone, the graduation, the promotion, the championship win, but almost no one prepares us for the emotional complexity that follows.

- What happens when the moment doesn't feel as triumphant as we expected?
- What do we do when success feels isolating?
- How do we navigate the space between who we were and who we are becoming?

Lonely Graduation isn't just about academic achievements. It's about the quiet, often disorienting, transitions we all face. It deep dives into the feeling of crossing a finish line only to realize that another race is about to begin.

Through my own experiences and the stories of others, this book explores the intersection of success and solitude, expectation and reality, achievement, and identity.

We'll break down the emotional stages of transition, the pressures of external validation, and the importance of redefining success on our own terms.

Who This Book Is For

This book is for anyone who has ever worked relentlessly toward a goal, only to feel unexpectedly lost once they reached it. It's for:

- First-generation college graduates who are navigating uncharted territory without a roadmap.
- High achievers who have checked every box but still feel something is missing.
- Professionals and leaders who have climbed the ranks, only to find the view lonelier at the top.
- Anyone in transition, whether it's moving to a new city, starting a career, or stepping into a different phase of life.
- Anyone on the other side of a significant accomplishment.
- Parents struggling with their child who is verging on graduating from high school and entering their next chapter of life.

This book is for you if you've ever found yourself asking that familiar question: Now what?

Lonely Graduation would not exist without the wisdom and vulnerability of those willing to speak the truths hidden behind their milestones.

These voices reveal what the world often overlooks: that the real work begins after the ceremony, after the title, after the victory.

Their journeys invite us to redefine success, not as arrival, but as ongoing becoming.

I hope that you find validation, insight, and a sense of connection through reading these pages. I also hope you recognize that loneliness is not just a deficit; it can also be an asset. Most importantly, this book helps you navigate your own Lonely Graduation with more clarity, purpose, and grace.

So get ready. Buckle up.

Let's begin.

Voices of Lonely Graduation

Emille Bryant

Emille Bryant is a consultant, strategist, and award-winning Air Force veteran whose mission is to change the world, one person and one idea at a time. As President and Founder of go:IKIGAI LLC, Emille helps individuals and organizations align their lives with a more profound sense of purpose, believing that true success begins with clarity of one's calling. Here, Emille reminds us that leadership is primarily not about accolades or positions. It is about living intentionally, loving fiercely, and blessing those who walk beside and after us.

Ifeomasinachi Ike

Often called Ifeoma or "Ify", she is an award-winning advocate, movement lawyer, and cultural strategist whose work bridges disciplines, industries, and global movements. Founder and Chief Equity Weaver of Pink Cornrows, Ifeoma challenges us to perceive success not as separation, but rather as an opportunity for radical reconnection and impact. Here, Ify reminds us that courage often lies not just in visible achievement, but instead in birthing imperfect work that transforms systems and centers community.

Malla Haridat

An award-winning entrepreneur, author, and founder of New Designs for Life, an innovative training company dedicated to fostering entrepreneurial thinking. A first-generation graduate of Columbia University, she shares her journey, demonstrating the complexities of elite spaces while staying rooted in community empowerment. Her perspective shows us that true healing and legacy do not emerge from individual success alone, but from lifting others along the climb.

Devin Johnson

Devin Johnson is a media executive with more than 30 years of experience in sports, digital media, and entertainment. From his tenure with NBCU and beyond, he has had roles or business relationships with most major entertainment companies in Hollywood. His most recent role was President of The SpringHill Company, the media and production company founded by LeBron James and Maverick Carter. A seasoned digital media executive and proud graduate of the University of Michigan and Duke University's Fuqua School of Business, Devin has led global brand expansion while remaining grounded in family and community. His reflections reveal that real achievement is not simply about professional milestones; it is about staying rooted, honest, and human through every personal and professional evolution.

Dennis S. Ellis

Dennis S. Ellis is a partner at Ellis George LLP, a premier litigation and trial law firm based in Los Angeles, known for its high-stakes legal advocacy and deep-rooted commitment to justice, innovation, and community engagement. A graduate of California State University, Fullerton, and Howard University School of Law, Dennis's journey reflects a relentless spirit: daring greatly, standing tall through wins and losses, and fighting forward even when the odds are unfavorable. He gives voice to the unseen battles behind success, those of belonging, resilience, and living with integrity in an often unfair world.

Kevan Turman

Kevan Turman is a God-fearing family man, a seasoned university advancement leader, and a passionate cultivator of community and opportunity. Currently serving as Vice Chancellor for University Advancement at Winston-Salem State University, Kevan's true calling is pouring into the growth of others, particularly young men seeking their fullest potential. Kevan reminds us that success without soul is hollow, and that living aligned with purpose is what truly sets the spirit on fire.

Dr. Kathleen Lawton-Trask

Dr. Kathleen Lawton-Trask is a scholar, writer, and educator whose work spans literature, creative writing, and cultural inquiry. A graduate of Swarthmore College, Columbia University, and the University of Oxford, Kathleen's pursuit of academic excellence is equal to her quiet rebelliousness and deep creative spirit. Kathleen reminds us that true identity is often forged not in moments of applause but in the spaces between them, where reflection, persistence, and quiet courage take root.

Benje M. Douglas

Benje Douglas is the Senior Vice President for Inclusion and Diversity at Bowdoin College. With a background in Title IX leadership and equity work, Benje centers belonging as a practice of humanity where people are free to show up fully without having to perform excellence. His approach to leadership is rooted in kindness, community, and the belief that healing and justice begin with each of us seeing one another clearly. In his words:

> *"We have to be kind to ourselves first, and kind to each other in equal measure."*

Why these voices?

I know many people from a variety of professions and spaces who could contribute to this book. I believe these voices are the ones that God wants you to hear in this configuration at this time in your life. Journal prompts are provided at the end of the book to add your reflections. Please take the conversations to a new level in your heart, home, and in dialogue with me, your colleagues, and the world.

You may become fans of some of the people this book introduces you to, and all of our lives can be enriched.

Let's keep going!

Defining Loneliness

Loneliness is a deeply personal and multifaceted emotional experience. Not simply the state of being alone, it is the painful gap between the relationships we have and the more meaningful, affirming connections we crave. Research consistently shows that loneliness emerges from a mismatch between desired human connections and actual social relationships (Botha & Bower, 2024; Bruss, Seth, & Zhao, 2024).

In fact, let's pause here and try an exercise. Take a breath and set the intention to ask some internal questions (and answer them). Can you recall one of your earliest feelings of being lonely? How far back can you go over the course of your life?

In my childhood, and perhaps yours, life was structured so that, at a minimum, I'd always have a parent checking in on me or reminding me to complete tasks. So, the most salient memory I have of being lonely was on my eighteenth birthday. My family, as always, acknowledged my birthday, but our financial resources didn't result in a new car in the driveway or an elaborate party. It was in the evening when loneliness began to set in. I'm not sure why, but I didn't particularly market my upcoming birthday to my friends, and I can't recall my circle celebrating with much intention. I wanted, however, to be connected and, of course, out of the house. So I went to "the block." Where I grew up, as elsewhere, it was the base where this large circle of friends would gather, known as a "click." So on "the block", we would spend time outside of Peetie and Ced's house before or after parties, and sometimes just spend hours hanging out all together. Perhaps I'll explain the context of the bonds made within our click in a different book, but what I knew was that I'd be welcomed. So I brought a small bottle of alcohol and went to "the block" and stopped at Peetie's. I was welcomed inside the house and shared that it was my birthday with the four or so friends that were already there; they celebrated with me in a relaxed manner. They hadn't known my birthday was coming up, but when I showed up needing my celebration, they were able to share the moment with me and essentially help me take care of myself. We drank, laughed, told stories, and just spent time together.

The moment before taking that action was lonely. I wanted to celebrate in relation to other people, but I had to know what I needed and pursue a route to get there. That was my earliest memory of loneliness. I've got plenty of other stories about feeling lonely when I didn't take action. I hope your reflection allows you to return to your body and the feelings that accompanied that experience. We'll need that sensory moment and many others as we proceed.

In the context of *Lonely Graduation*, loneliness often surfaces precisely at the intersection of success and transition, revealing emotional gaps beneath external accomplishments.

Loneliness can manifest in varied contexts, personal relationships, professional roles, leadership transitions, and various celebratory moments. As Devin Johnson noted,

> *"You can have the biggest, best job in the world, but when you get there, you realize there's always another step."*

His reflection underscores a hard truth: success does not eliminate loneliness; in many cases, it deepens it (Nie, Chen, & Yu, 2023).

In fact, in my conversation with Devin, I asked him the first question I asked everyone in this book: "How does the phrase' lonely graduation resonate with you?" Devin responded, "It doesn't." I thought, "Oh damn." Yet again, I hadn't considered the alternate reality of my own perspective, but that's why a scholar does their research! As we talked further, he asked me questions as I asked him questions. He shared with me how his journey wasn't a first-generation experience. It was a second-generation experience where he also saw his older brother go off to college. For Devin, college was expected; he likened it to a conveyor belt, a gradual journey to a well-prepared and informed end. As we unpacked that, the insights surfaced. I began to discover that the phrase "lonely graduation" was one I was using on its face, but it didn't mean the same for everyone. However, the more I examined my conversations for this book, the more I returned to honor various transitions.

Workplace and academic transitions, such as graduation or promotion, often introduce emotional disconnections, especially when achievements are not met with anticipated emotional support. Emille Bryant captures this phenomenon, saying,

> *"Nobody prepares you to be the only Black in the office. You're on an island, and nobody says you're on an island."*

This section explores the different dimensions of loneliness: its emotional and social facets, the hidden loneliness masked by success, and the psychological toll of significant transitions.

Emotional vs. Social Loneliness

Loneliness is not a singular experience but one that can emerge over time. It can be categorized into two primary forms: emotional loneliness and social loneliness.

Emotional loneliness occurs when an individual lacks deep, meaningful relationships that offer emotional validation and support.

As a school leader, I've observed and been tasked with creating programs to help students struggling with the impact of emotional loneliness. The first-year experience (FYE) programs often try to engage first-year college students within the first six weeks of the academic year to normalize bonding and movement around campus. The aim is to help students establish new connections while preventing isolation, which is a factor in poor graduation outcomes. As a dean, we would meet with our entire caseload of two hundred or so students within the first six weeks to break the ice. One of the most important questions I'd ask them was, "If you were having a bad day and I saw you, how would I know?" This question helped set the dynamic between the students and me because they would allow themselves to tell me what their respective cries for help looked like. I could then be a resource to them on both good and bad days. My days as a dean at Scripps and Bowdoin College were among the most memorable of my career!

I also knew someone in undergrad who served as a source of validation and connection, my mentor, Dr. Cheryl T. Chatman. To be brief, Dr. Chatman is a legend. This statement was verified by the City of St Paul, Minnesota, which proclaimed August 17th as Cheryl T. Chatman Day. It was Dr. Chatman who authentically saw me, this single-parent, student-athlete, as a scholar with potential. I would visit her office every day because she had "the good candy." I'm talking Twix, Twizzlers, Snickers—just about everything in three containers on the filing cabinet as you walked into her office. I stumbled upon this stash after I accompanied her back from the theater to her office in February 2002. She said she wanted to thank me for introducing a speaker earlier that morning for Black History Month. I had only been on campus for two weeks after transferring from my community college as a student-athlete. Apparently, the person who was supposed to execute the task got nervous. She looked in my direction in the tunnel under our academic buildings. The tunnel allowed everyone to move about campus without going outside in the snow, and since I had on a shirt with a collar, I should be able to do just fine. It was that call to action that sparked a lifesaving connection for me.

My connection with Dr. Chatman occurred in Week Two of the first six weeks of school. Having an encounter with the school's Executive Vice President & Dean of Diversity was life-changing, but at the time, it was the candy that kept me coming back!

I would visit her office and eat three to seven pieces of candy while sitting there before or after class. Eventually, my peers inquired about my abundance of confectionery corn syrup. Then word spread, and her office was regularly pretty full. That's where I learned how to be a school administrator. I would watch her work. I wouldn't know if she was having a bad day because she always held genuine conversations with anyone while still working. Under her advice, I began to apply for scholarships, join the student of color mentoring program, present to the grant foundation that funded the mentoring program, and eventually work at the university. Dr. Chatman's impact on my life was powerful. I didn't know that I needed a guide or to be seen, but I knew she believed in me, and deep down, I always believed in myself. The emotional connection allowed me to flourish. I never felt emotional loneliness in that space. I did witness it from others.

While this same school with access to the same resources (people, programs, etc), my teammates on the football team were struggling. I had come to St Paul from Southern California, following in the footsteps of two other teammates from my community college who transferred the year before. I had friends at school before I even arrived, but others from Florida, Chicago, and even Minneapolis struggled. My own friends from California struggled. Many people who move from the athletic spotlight at home must start over at the collegiate level. With much less structure than in high school, many of my peers didn't find the emotional connection with a school leader that I did (although several did), and, as a result, they found themselves reinforcing habits that eventually led to their detriment.

Emotional loneliness is the feeling of being unseen or misunderstood even when surrounded by others (Patel, Stentz, & Cougle, 2024; Sease et al., 2024). As Emille Bryant shared,

> *You can be surrounded by people but still be starved for someone who truly sees you, understands you, without the mask you have to wear.*

Social loneliness, by contrast, stems from the absence of consistent social ties or networks, particularly during life transitions like graduating from college or entering new professional spheres (Calderon Leon et al., 2024; Stocker et al., 2020).

For first-generation graduates, professionals, and leaders, both forms often collide. Malla Haridat, an entrepreneur and community advocate, reflected on her college years at Columbia University after realizing she was there for networking, not just for the degree.

Her realization illuminates a key aspect of *Lonely Graduation*: without an inherited blueprint for building social networks, many graduates find themselves academically accomplished yet socially isolated, unsure how to navigate the unspoken rules of post-graduation success (Chhajer, Chaudhry, & Mishra, 2024).

The Hidden Loneliness Within Success

Success is often portrayed as the antidote to struggle, yet research suggests that achievement can introduce its own profound isolation. The pursuit of excellence usually demands sacrifices, particularly relational ones, that result in emotional depletion (Yang, Lin, Chen, & Peng, 2023). High achievers frequently find themselves in environments where few share their experiences, leading to a more profound sense of disconnection (Nichols & McBride, 2017).

Ify Ike, advocate, lawyer, and strategist, eloquently described this phenomenon:

> *"Every time there is a graduation or some type of elevation, it makes you more removed from community."*

I've experienced the necessary adjustment in upward mobility. In leadership roles, this removal is exacerbated by the shifting expectations and pressures associated with professional advancement (Dor-Haim, 2023; Jin & Ikeda, 2024).

Kevan Turman reflected on this dynamic:

> *"The higher you go, the fewer people you have who can actually see you as human and not just as a title."*

Kevan's observation rings true within my experience.

As a Black man in an executive role, I've experienced how constituents can advocate for their needs while ignoring my own personhood and how the circumstances of the world may also be impacting me on an empathetic level. Case in point, when George Floyd was murdered, my school organized conversations and spaces to process for faculty and staff. Yet, as a director tasked with the charge, my peers didn't express that they might need to check on me, as a Black man. I've also experienced parents advocating for their students while making invalidating statements and comments as they compared our institutional responses to be lacking by only comparing them to how we would respond if the person involved were Black. Microaggressions in this form occur all the time. Spending time to disrupt the bias at play can offload an insurmountable amount of labor, also mine to process, and be more productive than compartmentalizing the impact. It's as if my individual identity dissolves into a professional role.

Success, then, does not always fill the void of support offered for someone in their new form of self-actualization; it can widen it.

As research by Botha and Bower (2024) suggests, loneliness can persist, and even intensify, across adult life stages if meaningful social connections are not actively cultivated.

This chasm between external validation and internal fulfillment forms the core of the *Lonely Graduation* experience. As Devin Johnson poignantly summarized.:

> *"It's the dissonance between the image of success and the private experience of isolation."*

I recall a moment when I was taking on more responsibility at work, and my peers applauded the shift and the resulting promotion as I transitioned from a lateral peer to a supervisor. There was a level of connection that made the choice comfortable and safe because it was actually a predictable move. I had earned the team's trust, and we were in it together. I contrast that moment with another elevation I received while working for a different organization. There, the response from my peers was essentially flat and unacknowledged. Having had the first experience made the second experience very loud. Devin said, "the experience of elevation was very lonely." I agree with that statement. In my situation, it would've been inappropriate to attempt to unpack my feelings of a lack of reaction to what should've been a congratulatory moment for a colleague. I understood this because, in a hierarchical system that elevated someone in the organizational chart among peers, the upward movement had shifted the power dynamics from the existing lateral structure. I've often said leadership is lonely because, as a leader, you have more information and authority than most, or at least several others in your orbit. This means you must express even less than you know on a matter, out of your own psychological sustainability at times. This stems from the weight and magnitude of the decisions you're called to make. So as you ascend into your success, becoming a steward of your light and gifts can feel hard to manage. Not because you aren't capable, but because of how the world around you adjusts to your journey. Everyone who clapped when you won a silver medal doesn't do so when you win a gold one. Some would even prefer that you didn't.

The Emotional Toll of Transition

Transitions, whether from student to graduate, employee to leader, or one life stage to another, often bring unexpected waves of loneliness. These pivotal moments require a recalibration of identity, relationships, and purpose, frequently leaving individuals unmoored (Calderon Leon et al., 2024; Pavlova & Bannikov, 2015). For me, the pivot is always an emotional one. When my family and I left California for Maine in 2014. My oldest son was starting boarding school in Mid-Coast Maine, which was the reason I even searched for work in that state. His opportunity turned out to be a massive opportunity for me as well. My wife was on the fence about his attending a boarding school so far from his father's presence. She preferred us to be a bit closer if we could. I began looking for jobs in the region and found one at Bowdoin College as an Assistant Dean of Student Affairs. The role was a step up professionally and placed us about forty miles away from where my son would attend school. I was excited to blaze a new trail.

The transition resulted in us leaving our home church, which our family had been members of since 2007. Our farewell was beautiful. The entire church prayed for our family. The leadership and congregation gifted us with an outpouring of appreciation for our family; we were able to return that appreciation to our church family as well. We did not know how deep those relationships were until we had to reckon with moving on. It was a sad feeling due to love and connection that would be missed. The sadness I felt as I said farewell to our church is not rooted in regret, but in the profound realization that public milestones or opportunities, such as professional growth or education, do not necessarily deliver the emotional rewards privately anticipated.

Did the sadness make us want to stay? No. It did drive us to find the feeling in Maine. That just did not happen. The formidable lack of connection to our new home led us to decide to move back to California after a year. We had grown. Our needs had changed, and then changed again. The year apart allowed us to gain some perspective. During that time, we made other choices to continue developing spiritually in different ways and to avoid returning to our previous church.

Transitions also dismantle the structured environments, schools, athletic teams, and workplaces that once provided emotional and social anchoring. Without these communal frameworks, individuals often drift into an emotional liminality, a suspended and often discomforting space between who they were and who they are becoming.

Research on perceived stress and loneliness (Wang et al., 2024) indicates that disruptions to sleep, coping mechanisms, and social supports during transition periods exacerbate depressive symptoms and emotional exhaustion.

Moreover, external expectations placed on individuals navigating transitions can compound internal uncertainty.

Malla Haridat vividly captured this pressure:

> *"You're the one looked at in your family as the beacon of light and hope, but you don't have a clue what to do next."*

When the weight of others' hopes collides with one's own disorientation, loneliness sharpens. The need for intentional emotional processing becomes critical.

Emille Bryant underscores the necessity of this inquiry:

> *"Processing gives you the ability to stay on course. It's not to solve or resolve, it's simply to stay functional amidst the turmoil."*

Loneliness, then, is not simply a temporary side effect of success or transition; it is a fundamental emotional terrain that must be acknowledged, navigated, and integrated into the journey toward wholeness.

Summary

Loneliness is a layered, complex phenomenon that intensifies at the crossroads of achievement and identity shift. Through the lived experiences of *Lonely Graduation* participants, it becomes clear that the external markers of success do not immunize against emotional isolation. Instead, they often magnify the quiet, unmet longing for connection, understanding, and authentic community. By understanding loneliness not as a personal failure, but rather as an inevitable companion of transformation, we can create new models of support that honor both individual excellence and collective belonging.

Defining Graduation

Graduation is often imagined as the triumphant final step of an academic journey, a public ceremony marking the completion of a course of study. Yet, such graduations are far more than events. They symbolize and are a profound emotional and developmental transition: a threshold between who we were, who we are, and who we are still becoming (Calderon Leon et al., 2024; Montana State University, n.d.).

While graduation represents achievement, growth, and the fulfillment of dreams, its emotional meaning extends well beyond the conferral of a diploma. Graduation is not just an arrival. It is an emotional recalibration, a redefinition of self, belonging, and purpose, that demands far more than is publicly acknowledged.

While achievements like graduation are often outwardly celebrated, they can simultaneously trigger hidden feelings of disconnection, loss, and vulnerability in those graduating. For many, graduation carries the belief that crossing the stage will deliver stability, success, and belonging. However, the lived reality often reveals a more complicated emotional terrain where support systems shift, identities evolve, and uncertainty quietly grows beneath the surface.

Please note that graduation comes in many formats. Relocating to a new part of the country, ending a relationship, and many other transitions exemplify these. Let's extend the symbolism of graduation across the spectrum of life's moments. In doing so, we might uncover how we've navigated the closing of chapters in our lives.

More than a Ceremony: Graduation as Transformation

Graduation functions as a rite of passage, an anthropological and psychological milestone structured around three phases: separation, transition, and incorporation (Sease et al., 2024; Calderon Leon et al., 2024).

In this framework, graduation marks the **transition stage**, a time of emotional instability, role confusion, and deep searching for new forms of belonging.

More than the culmination of coursework or the acquisition of credentials, it is the symbolic disassembly of a prior identity and the tentative assembly of a new one. Yet, the moment, event, or day itself often fails to deliver the transformative emotional payoff so many expect.

Malla Haridat captured this tension when she reflected:

> *"Nobody ever tells you about the moment after the moment. The journey is always the journey, but then once it's there, you gotta figure out what you're going to be doing after that."*

Graduation ceremonies emphasize closure and completion, but offer little guidance for what lies ahead.

Research on college transition loneliness confirms that former students' greatest emotional vulnerability often arises after the celebration ends, when they face an uncertain world stripped of the structured safety nets they once relied on (Calderon Leon et al., 2024; Stocker et al., 2020).

Graduation, therefore, is both a celebratory and a disorienting moment.

It honors the labor, persistence, and sacrifice that brought students to the threshold, but it also signals the beginning of a new, unstructured journey of becoming.

What We Expect vs. What We Experience

For most who make their way into higher education, success is much like a roadmap: graduate high school, attend college, earn a degree or two, and obtain a stable career. Each milestone is framed as a predictable stepping stone to security and belonging.

But what happens when the lived experience of accomplishment does not align with these expectations?

Devin Johnson reflected on this jarring realization:

> *"My friend and I thought if we ever made $100,000, life was over. That was it. We'd be rich. We'd have whatever car we wanted. But then you get there and you realize... oh."*

This gap between expectation and reality is well documented.

Studies show that during major life transitions, the collapse of familiar social and emotional support systems often leads to disillusionment, loneliness, and emotional distress despite external achievements (Bruss, Seth, & Zhao, 2024; Wang & Zeng, 2024).

For first-generation graduates, this collapse can be felt more deeply and is often more emotionally fraught.

Malla Haridat described the hidden curriculum she encountered during her undergraduate journey:

> *"All the things that I didn't know, that I didn't know, that I didn't know... you could say that about four times over, and each time matters as a first-gen college graduate."*

Without access to pre-planned social scripts for navigating post-graduation life, networking, accessing opportunities, and sustaining emotional resilience, first-generation graduates must forge their own uncertain paths, often without the safety nets, such as being able to come home and reset for a period of time without having to earn or provide for others (Chhajer, Chaudhry, & Mishra, 2024).

The emotional cost of graduation lies not only in the celebration of what has been achieved but also in the often-solitary reconstruction of life that follows.

The Aftermath of Accomplishment

Graduation marks the end of one chapter, but it rarely offers a clear beginning to the next.

It is in the aftermath, when the ceremony gives way to silence, that the actual emotional weight of accomplishment settles.

This sadness is not rooted in regret. Instead, it arises from the profound realization that external achievements do not automatically fulfill internal emotional needs for connection, purpose, and belonging.

As research from Nicholas Pang (2022) and Montana State University (n.d.) shows, many graduates report feelings of disconnection, identity confusion, and grief as they leave behind familiar communities, structures, and roles.

Even professional success mirrors this cycle. Devin Johnson reflected on reaching an early career salary milestone, noting that "it isn't a magical marker...the gates of heaven don't open when you cross it."

This mirrors the post-graduation reality for so many decorated scholars: No matter how far one climbs, the next level demands further adaptation, resilience, and emotional recalibration.

Success is not a static destination; it is an ongoing negotiation with new challenges, new responsibilities, and new forms of loneliness.

Graduation, often portrayed as a culmination with a climactic ending, is in truth the beginning of an uncharted emotional journey.

It demands that individuals continually redefine achievement for themselves, build new support systems from scratch, and develop emotional tools strong enough to weather the inevitable, often ongoing, dissonance between public success and private experience.

Summary

Graduation is a complex, transitional rite of passage. It is not simply the culmination of educational achievement or career attainment, but the beginning of an emotional, relational, and identity-based reorientation.

For many, the ceremony offers closure for one chapter while opening up profound uncertainties for the next.

The voices in *Lonely Graduation* remind us that beyond the applause and regalia, there is a deeper journey, one that demands resilience, intentional reflection, and a radical reimagining of what it means to succeed and to belong.

The Intersection of Loneliness and Graduation

At first glance, graduation and loneliness seem like opposing experiences, one a celebration of achievement, the other an emotional state of isolation. Yet in reality, they are deeply and intricately connected, shaping how individuals experience and endure transitions, milestones, and the profound emotional terrain of personal transformation.

Research consistently shows that significant life transitions, such as graduating from college, frequently precipitate heightened loneliness due to the abrupt loss of structured social networks (affinity groups, clubs, teams), identity anchors (first-gen students, international students), and familiar roles (resident assistant, intern, graduate assistant) (Calderon Leon et al., 2024; Stocker et al., 2020). Graduation, while symbolizing resilience, effort, and growth, simultaneously initiates a subtle but potent emotional rupture: the "moment after the moment."

As Montana State University Counseling Services notes, the post-graduation period can evoke unexpected feelings of loss, confusion, and isolation, even when external markers of success, such as awards, promotions, and praise, are abundant (Montana State University, n.d.). The stability, support, and communal bonds that once undergirded academic life often fail to meet one in the next phase of life.

Instead, graduates may find themselves navigating a landscape of exhilarating potential that remains disorienting because of its unfamiliar structure.

This unsettling realization, that reaching a long-awaited goal can trigger profound emotional disconnection, is the essence of what *Lonely Graduation* seeks to name and explore.

As Ify shared with us, transition and graduation can remove us from the community. Research shows that academic and professional elevations, such as promotions, pay increases, and management responsibilities, frequently increase emotional distance from familiar support systems, even as they elevate social status or professional standing (Nichols & McBride, 2017; Jin & Ikeda, 2024).

Loneliness at this stage is not merely about physical distance from friends, classmates, or mentors.

This state of stagnation or freefall is the emotional and existential distance created by changing expectations, evolving identities, and the silent loss of shared experiences within a group or cohort designed to enable communal progression.

In this way, the very ceremony meant to celebrate achievement simultaneously marks the beginning of profound emotional isolation.

The Gap Between Expectation and Reality

Throughout our lives, success is presented as a linear, upward trajectory: complete one milestone, move seamlessly to the next, and with each step, accumulate greater security, belonging, and fulfillment.

Graduation is often framed as the crowning jewel of this journey, the promised reward for years of perseverance and sacrifice.

Yet what happens when the reality of life after graduation diverges sharply from these promises?

Studies confirm that milestone transitions, especially those weighted with high expectations, often precipitate feelings of loneliness, sadness, and vulnerability when outcomes fall short of internalized hopes (Pang, 2022; Wang et al., 2024).

Graduates are often unprepared for the emotional aftermath of "successful" achievement.

The roadmap ends at graduation, but the journey forward is uncharted, with few guideposts.

Instead of triumphant certainty, many experience a sense of drift between what was expected and what is now real.

For first-generation graduates, this gap between expectation and reality can feel especially vast.

While degrees are intended to unlock opportunity, many first-generation graduates encounter hidden systemic barriers around networking, professional advancement, and emotional support.

Malla Haridat highlights the "hidden curriculum"-the unspoken rules, societal and professional assumptions, and social capital that privileged students inherit, but which first-generation students must piece together on their own (Chhajer, Chaudhry, & Mishra, 2024; Calderon Leon et al., 2024).

When external celebrations end and internal doubts surface, many graduates are left wrestling with logistical uncertainties and profound emotional dislocation.

Behavioral research reveals that unmet expectations around success correlate strongly with increased psychological vulnerability, including loneliness, depression, and maladaptive coping mechanisms such as emotional withdrawal and excessive online escapism (Wang & Zeng, 2024; Patel, Stentz, & Cougle, 2024).

Thus, graduation is not simply an ending.

It is a collision between personal expectation and institutional completion, a moment when triumph and turmoil coexist, when public validation masks private uncertainty, and when the journey toward becoming truly begins.

Summary

The intersection of loneliness and graduation reveals emotional undercurrents, such as the recalibration of one's identity or the loss of institutional support that has yet to be processed; however, it can be masked by celebration and ceremony.

While graduation is framed publicly as a joyful endpoint, privately it often marks the beginning of a profound emotional recalibration, one that demands not only professional resilience but also profound personal reckoning, which includes the recalibration of a sense of self once we realize that the path is never linear.

Lonely Graduation challenges the dominant narrative that achievement equates to fulfillment.

It reminds us that even amid accolades, individuals must navigate the silent grief of transition, the invisible work of identity reconstruction, which includes the emotional labor of exploring beliefs and social roles, and the unspoken yearning for meaningful connection with people who empathize with and energize you in the wake of public success.

Graduation is not the finish line it appears to be.

It is the threshold of a new, complex, and emotionally rich journey, one rarely named yet deeply felt.

PART II

THE EMOTIONAL STAGES OF LONELY GRADUATION

Graduation is marketed as the ultimate reward for perseverance, a moment when hard work finally pays off, when dreams materialize into tangible success, and when a theorized sense of fulfillment is supposed to settle in. Yet for many, the reality of post-graduation life reveals a much more complicated emotional landscape.

The emotional stages of *Lonely Graduation* detailed in this section trace the gap between expectation and reality, the exhaustion of unexamined achievement, and the urgent need to redefine success from within rather than without.

Success:
Expectation vs. Reality

Growing up, expectations were set early in my home to be successful, and college was always part of that narrative. My parents always preached that I would graduate from college, but not in an overbearing way. It felt as if they were speaking about the developmental stages of youth. While neither of my parents graduated from college, they are both intelligent and understand the significance of the milestone. I felt no negative pressure from them in that regard. Fortunately, I was a decent student, and my eventual graduation seemed inevitable as long as I continued to make progress toward the plan my advisors laid out. However, my family was unaware of what to expect as a college student. The unawareness showed in my preparation for the journey. Knowing the social and intellectual value of college while lacking the tools to navigate the path, I was left to figure it out as best I could by building and flying my plane at the same time.

Graduation was always spoken of as the dream on the hill, and we never actually got around to discussing life after degree attainment with any seriousness. In fact, once I was admitted to college, the familial conversation about completing a degree actually stopped. It was as if I had already achieved the dream.

The feeling and intensity of finishing was something that I carried alone. I stopped visiting home after my second year and began to make my life in the Twin Cities. I was an adult. However, as a young parent entering my final year of eligibility as a student-athlete, I spoke with my advisor about my path to degree completion. I was an education major on paper with a concentration in physical education. No part of me wanted to pursue that path, but that was the track my coaches had placed me on years prior when I enrolled at Riverside Community College as a freshman. But I digress. Heading into my last year, I told my advisor that I needed to graduate in the spring. We discovered that if that was my goal, I could graduate with a degree in kinesiology, which would require a practicum and some additional units over the next 18 months. Safe to say the rest is history. I did what I needed to do to finish.

I met the expectation of success, but the reality of what it took to get there and the aftermath that emerged were books from two different genres.

From an early age, I was taught that success follows a simple, linear formula: study hard, graduate, secure a good job, and everything will fall neatly into place. Graduation is framed as the apex of this journey, the golden key to opportunity, security, and belonging.

Yet many graduates quickly discover that reaching the milestone does not automatically deliver the fulfillment they expected.

Instead, the moment often prompts an unsettling question: *Now what?*

The emotional whiplash between public celebration and private emptiness is jarring.

Rather than feeling anchored, many graduates feel unmoored, standing at the summit only to realize the horizon has shifted once again. I recall this feeling being communicated to my peers in my doctoral program. A week or so after graduation, I spoke with a friend of mine, and she said she felt accomplished yet a bit hesitant about what to do at this stage. She was unsure whether she should try to publish her findings, continue researching alone, or just look for a job.

This disconnect between expectation and lived experience is a hallmark of *Lonely Graduation*, revealing how milestone achievements, divorced from deeper meaning or emotional anchoring, can paradoxically deepen loneliness rather than alleviate it.

The Conveyor Belt of Achievement

For high achievers, graduation can feel less like a climactic accomplishment and more like another obligatory checkpoint on an endless, in-motion list of expectations.

Devin Johnson reflected on this numbing progression:

> *"It felt like a conveyor belt, like I was just checking all the boxes. Graduation didn't feel like an accomplishment. It was just one step on my way to adulthood."*

The culture of perpetual striving leaves little space to honor, grieve, or even truly process success.

The next goal, the following metric, and the next societal expectation quickly eclipse each achievement.

As a result, even monumental milestones, like graduating from college, earning a significant promotion, or reaching a long-held financial goal, may feel oddly anticlimactic.

I, too, have felt the out-of-body and anticlimactic feeling as a professional. After a lengthy interview process to advance within an organization, I was underwhelmed by the salary and benefits of the new role. At that point in my career, it was an outstanding achievement, but the spoils didn't meet my expectations. It wasn't the last time I had that feeling either.

The emotional toll of achievement without pause is profound.

When accomplishment becomes a reflexive, expected outcome rather than a meaningful victory, individuals are left vulnerable to exhaustion, emotional detachment, and a creeping sense of emptiness.

For Dennis Ellis, lonely graduation was not metaphorical; it was literal, visceral, and devastating. He remembered the day his family came to his law school graduation:

> *"They gave me a card with nothing in it, with no money, no nothing. And was just like, 'This is it. I'm glad you're no longer a burden.' Basically, no congratulations. I had honor cords, the whole thing, and it was just like nothing."*

That absence of affirmation cut deeply. It was not just about a missing gift or words of pride; it was the culmination of promises that had dissolved over the years.

> *"When I decided to go to Howard... my grandmother and mother said they would be supportive. And it quickly dissipated. And then this was the culmination of all of that... congratulations, get the hell off our backs."*

The result was isolation at the very moment when recognition should have felt richest. Instead of celebration, Dennis climbed into a late-model Ford Thunderbird and drove across the country, alone, to take the bar exam. He asked his mother if his brother could ride with him, but she refused.

> *"She said no. She said the reason was she wasn't going to pay for him to fly back... I was it. It was over. Completely done."*

On that drive, loneliness turned into something heavier.

> *"On that trip, I cried multiple times. I was depressed again, almost like when I lost my football career. I listened to music that was emotional... I must have listened to Donny Hathaway's 'Someday We'll All Be Free' a hundred times. If you ask me what my favorite song is in the world, that's my favorite song."*

This stage of lonely graduation, the collapse, wasn't just grief. It was the breaking of illusions that family support or external recognition would always catch him. And yet, out of that collapse came fuel.

When he reached California, Dennis turned his pain into intensity.

> *"I used all that depression, all that negativity, and I used it as my fuel... I stopped eating red meat, I worked out in the mornings. I probably lost 40 pounds while I was taking the bar. I just was focused on it all."*

There was no audience, no family cheering him on. Only one friend, Kelvin Ross, stood by him, offering a place to stay. Dennis studied in an attic, day after day at Berkeley's Boalt Hall, burning the ache into purpose.

He was clear that this was not triumphalism.

Shifting from External Validation to Internal Fulfillment

Many pursue academic and career success fueled by a desire for external validation, from parents, peers, mentors, or society at large.

The applause, the accolades, and the public recognition serve as temporary affirmations that the struggle was worth it.

But when the applause fades, as it inevitably does, graduates are left confronting a deeper, more unsettling question: *Was this success truly for me?*

Devin Johnson's reflection offers a glimpse into this reckoning:

> *"I wanted this to be my last job. I wanted to ride off into the sunset... but over time, things changed, and I started thinking, 'Maybe for the first time, I should take a job based on passion, not just paying bills."*

This moment signals a crucial emotional shift: the transition from chasing external validation toward cultivating internal fulfillment.

It is the realization that success, when defined solely by societal expectations or material benchmarks, cannot sustain meaning or belonging over time.

The real work of adulthood, and of emotional maturation, begins when individuals start questioning inherited definitions of success and construct new definitions rooted in passion, purpose, and authentic identity.

Being a workaholic isn't a badge of honor. Take that from someone who actually enjoys working. Now I don't know if that connection to work and joy could be subconsciously associated with the gender roles for men and the expectation of being a provider. I may be internalizing all of that, but as I said, I enjoy working. What I learned after I expected applause for working all those hours was that rest is best. For some, taking time off was taboo. I'm glad I've been released from that demon! I'll take a vacation in a minute. To me, taking time off, or simply planning the time you'll take off, is radical resistance against what's projected onto you and what you truly desire for yourself to recharge. The truth was that I avoided vacations and time off because I felt that my value was in my production. Once I became an authentic listener to my spirit, I uncovered my own ebbs and flows of the work and rest cycle. I learned that I have two seasons of burnout a year, February and May. That has changed over the years, but since I know those moments are more challenging for me, I plan trips around spring break and summer to properly restore my spirit. These changes allowed me to be kinder to myself and others. I don't feel ashamed of using my time off or of what I choose to do with it. Sometimes it's a week enjoying bourbon and cigars, and other times it's warm water and the Caribbean with my wife. Find what your spirit needs to celebrate you and run toward it.

Lonely Graduation doesn't just concern the emotional aftermath of a ceremony; it is the beginning of this deeper inner journey, a journey that veers away from seeking external applause toward following an internal compass that asks not just *what I have achieved but also who I am becoming.*

I've known Benje Douglas for more than ten years. We met at Bowdoin College during our first few weeks of employment there. I ended up leaving after a year, and during my research for this book, Benje shared that my exit was a lonely graduation moment for him. What he confided to me carried the weight of disorientation but also the glimmer of insight, an awareness that loneliness isn't just a deficit, but can also be an asset.

He recalled how my leaving forced him to confront adulthood in a way that coursework or institutional expectations never could.

"It wasn't actually when you told me you were leaving. It was when you told me that you were wrapping up the summer a little bit earlier than you thought you were... That was adulthood personified, where I was like, sometimes you do things you don't like to get things you do want."

For Benje, that realization marked a rupture: the recognition that life might not consistently deliver a celebration at the end of hard work. Instead, the work itself stretches forward in perpetuity. He described it as the summer when he doubled down on staying in a place he didn't like because the trade-off was stability, money, and support.

"I hadn't really dawned on me that maybe your whole life is that... you just consistently go from assignment to assignment, and then you don't get a big celebration at the end [of each assignment]. You just keep on doing."

What made that transition sharper was the abrupt absence of our connection in a space that had already felt isolating.

"I didn't realize how emotionally tied I was to you until you said that you were leaving. I was like, dang. I can't quite fathom this place as white as it is without you in it."

That loss was compounded and complicated by the arrival and substitution of a colleague named Benjamin, who was hired around the same time. Benje remembered the absurdity of colleagues confusing them, as if sharing a first syllable in their names was enough to collapse individuality. The humor carried an edge: survival in these environments often meant erasure or conflation.

Yet even in that dissonance, Benje found an inflection point. He named it *"the beginning of an era,"* a moment that was both heavy and clarifying. Between my departure, his brother's visit that summer, and the long weekend they spent together, he began to glimpse the contours of adulthood not just as a burden but as responsibility, continuity, and, eventually, choice.

In this way, lonely graduation wasn't only about endings or abandonment. It was also about the dawning realization that transition itself is a teacher, stripping away illusions of constant affirmation and introducing the deeper work of resilience and self-definition.

Summary

The emotional stages of *Lonely Graduation* reveal that success is not a destination but a crucible.

It tests the narratives we were given, the metrics we inherited, and the expectations we internalized.

Graduation is not the end of striving; it is the moment when the striving itself must be questioned, deconstructed, and reimagined.

True fulfillment is found not in reaching a finish line, but in building a life aligned with one's deepest values, passions, and dreams, on one's own terms.

The Emotional Complexity of Transition

For some, major life transitions are accompanied by emotional turbulence.

Graduation, often portrayed as a definitive victory, initiates a journey not of arrival but of profound emotional dislocation and identity recalibration.

While the moment after graduation is filled with possibilities, it is equally saturated with uncertainty, vulnerability, and quiet grief for what is being left behind.

Graduates expect to experience joy, pride, and a clear sense of forward momentum. Instead, many encounter disorientation, the sudden collapse of structure, the evaporation of familiar social networks, and the disappearance of routines that once scaffolded their daily lives.

As Calderon Leon et al. (2024) and Montana State University (n.d.) affirm, these disruptions heighten the risk of loneliness during transitional periods, even amid public celebrations of success.

Malla Haridat captured the layered complexity of this experience in realizing that she didn't know what she didn't know.

Her insight points to the hidden dimensions of transition: the emotional, logistical, and social knowledge gaps that often remain invisible until the moment they are most needed.

In these gaps, loneliness festers not just from the absence of people but from the overwhelming realization that the roadmap promised to graduates was incomplete, selective, and at times illusory.

For Ify Ike, the publication of her first book, "The Equity Mindset", was supposed to be a graduation, a visible, celebratory marker of achievement. Yet the reality was dissonant.

> *"On certain metrics, it was a graduation... technically it's published, technically it's out there in the world, technically it was on bestseller lists. But I still think I'm a Journey Girl."*

The milestone felt hollow because the process was fraught with illness, pressure, and neglect. Writing under the weight of long COVID, she had to wrestle with occasional short-term memory loss and fatigue even as deadlines loomed.

> *"This publisher wants you to graduate. They want you to publish this book. And then you're facing the expectations of other people again, another moment where the graduation means something else, more to somebody else other than me."*

She recalled the indifference vividly:

> *"They didn't care how lonely, they didn't care how insecure, they didn't care that I wasn't well. They didn't even care enough to send me a version of my book before it was published."*

The result was estrangement from her own work, what she called *"a very lonely graduation."* In her reflection, Ify returned to the image of time. Unlike a traditional graduation, which is scheduled, measured, and bound by institutional calendars, she has to redefine a sense of completion for herself.

> *"The one thing that's fixed at times around graduation is time, you're on someone else's time. But when an individual defines graduation for themselves, the molding of it is not time. It's process, it's milestones, it's the journey."*

The costs of surrendering control were sobering: giving away too much of her intellectual property, losing trust in the publishing process, and realizing too late the lessons other authors had modeled.

"I shouldn't have called it '*The Equity Mindset,* '" she admitted, noting how other thought leaders protected their creations by naming their books differently. In Ify's case, "The Equity Mindset" is her IP, and entering into the dynamic with her publisher made her feel like she'd given a piece of it away. The frustration of seeing her life's work, something she coined and embodied, contracted into someone else's ledger became part of the lonely graduation itself.

And yet, Ify also named the assets hidden in that pain.

> *"As much as the framing sounds like it's a deficit, lonely graduation. I believe there is asset in the experience. If you achieve the state of lonely graduation, congratulations, you've done it. There are things you feel when you complete—like a race— relief, reflection, the recognition that only you can tell your story."*

This reframing shifted her posture for the future. The point wasn't to emotionally or physically rewrite the disappointment of the first graduation, but to prepare differently for the next one.

> *"How you posture after achieving a thing could be the beginning of actually enjoying what you've achieved... Maybe creating intentional lonely graduations could be different than feeling like you fell into an unpleasant one."*

Ify's story illuminates another stage of lonely graduation: the tension between ownership and expectation, the push to deliver for others while searching for authenticity within. Her words remind us that milestones that should be exciting achievements can become stolen graduations, leaving scars from significant times in our lives that rarely heal. The true work is reclaiming authorship, not just of the book one may publish, but of the meaning of the moment itself.

The Role of Reflection
in Processing Change

Transitions, particularly those like graduation, demand intentional reflection.

Without pausing to process the emotional weight of change, individuals can feel as if they are in freefall, tumbling through expectations, fears, and emerging realities without a parachute.

Yet sitting in stillness, facing the emotional turbulence rather than fleeing from it, is both difficult and necessary.

As Sease et al. (2024) note, reflection is essential for emotional regulation and meaning-making during periods of transition.

I can recall my 40th birthday. I just wanted to sit in a chair and think. It was one of those milestone birthdays, but I tapped into its significance. So, instead of walking into it and being hit by a wave of emotions, I chose deliberate silence, deliberate loneliness. I wanted the stillness of my thoughts. For the first time, I knew that there was an asset in pausing within the moment for myself. It allowed me to honor my internal rite of passage into my 40s and not perform for anyone. I was happy, proud, and at peace with myself.

These small moments, pausing to think, choosing to rest, often signal the beginning of a deeper internal reckoning.

Reflection, misunderstood by a culture obsessed with productivity, is not stagnation; it is the unseen labor of emotional integration and future alignment.

Without it, individuals risk perpetuating the conveyor belt of achievement without ever confronting whether the life they are building is the life they actually desire.

The Unseen Work Behind Success

Let me share with you some statistics from my collegiate football career. I do this because one, none of my children particularly care about these stats. Two, if I don't talk about them somewhere, I risk losing the opportunity to be my own version of Al Bundy, who scored four touchdowns in a single game, but I digress. You see, over two seasons of Division II NCAA football, I recorded six interceptions, sixty-four tackles, and a blocked field goal. I ranked in the all-time Top Ten for both pass breakups and blocked kicks at my school in Saint Paul, Minnesota, at the time of this publication. Now, what was my point in sharing all this information with you? Well, one, I had to work to be good enough to earn those stats.

I was pretty terrible at football in high school. In fact, I sat on the bench all four years except for my senior year, when I played sparingly after homecoming. I remember that transition because I had my first child, Chris, when I was seventeen years old. He was born a week before homecoming. The first game I suited up for after he was born was homecoming, and I had a new motivation as a father. I knew I needed to create a life that would allow me to be a good father, nurturing and providing for him. Football needed to become a resource that could help me do that. Four years early, I told myself this was the beginning of an era, yet I had never played football before, and there was no guarantee that I'd be good at it.

I kept practicing and working hard, eventually earning my way to play college football and receiving all-conference recognition. I ended up being a decent player, but nobody cared or knew about that backstory. My journey as a student-athlete serves as confirmation in my file of life that I sought out to achieve a goal and accomplished it. I can revisit my ability to achieve this goal and build on the memories of this private triumph. It's my example of self-motivation and accountability. What most people would hear from my student-athlete story could be, "oh you played college footbal", not the unseen work that went into that success. I need to have that understanding for myself.

I've got another story for you. I told you at the beginning of this book that I finished my PhD at the University of San Diego in the spring of 2025. I didn't share that this is my third attempt at obtaining a doctorate. Yep, that's right. Before accomplishing this feat, I had attempted and dropped out of programs twice. Statistically, there was no indication that I'd be successful this last time aside from my sheer, renewed commitment to literally succeeding.

Success narratives often valorize talent and perseverance, but they frequently obscure the vital roles of opportunity, access, and social capital in shaping outcomes.

As Yosso's (2005) research on *Community Cultural Wealth* emphasizes, access to social networks and relational capital can fundamentally alter life trajectories.

Devin Johnson offered a candid reflection on this unseen scaffolding:

> *"My brother knew somebody at NBCU. That one introduction changed my life."*

This brief, casual connection had a transformative impact, illustrating how opportunity often hinges on who you know, not just what you know.

For first-generation graduates and marginalized individuals, this invisible infrastructure can feel both elusive and exclusionary.

Without inherited networks or insider guidance, even those who achieve extraordinary things can find themselves adrift, aware that they are missing a level of self-actualization or an indicator that they are on the right track and unsure how to access it.

The hidden architecture of success magnifies loneliness by making systemic barriers seem like personal shortcomings rather than collective failures.

58

Christopher S. Dennis

The hidden architecture of success magnifies loneliness by making systemic barriers seem like personal shortcomings rather than collective failures.

Navigating Social Capital
Without a Roadmap

Each year, I facilitate a workshop on navigating your personal story as part of a college-essay workshop intensive that my school hosts for our high school seniors. During that workshop, I helped students examine layers of their identity across multiple social identifiers. Some of those identifiers include race, ethnicity, learning style, citizenship status, and family makeup. An element of identity that stands out concerns social and academic achievement. I help illustrate social achievement by providing examples for attendees. One is of the expectations heaped upon the person known for throwing the best parties.

In some cases, they are relied upon to be the happy-go-lucky kid who lives at the fun party house or a person to sustain that culture. It's like they are the class clown who people expect to never evolve into anything beyond the keeper of good fun and humor. But what happens when they no longer want to throw the party? Sometimes that person is met with anger, frustration, or judgment from their peers because they no longer wish to be known as a party animal. Similarly, the student known for getting stellar grades merges their internal identity with their social and academic recognition. This reaches the point that, if or when they no longer receive those notable grades (or see others do the same), they find themselves somewhat confused or dazed about who they really are without that achievement.

This is where social capital comes into sharper focus. Social capital is the value created through relationships, including access to opportunity, upward mobility, and the benefits that come from networks working on your behalf, even in your absence.

For some people, full awareness of social capital's impact on their life options drives them to strategically plan and navigate their lives, knowing that the stakes are high. For others, the expectations of enjoying the right happy hour, attending the right conferences, learning to send thank-you communications and other follow-ups, and playing the game of professional politics can be daunting.

As we enter the adolescence of the social media influencer craze, the social footprint each of us leaves behind often precedes us. This is a space that most young people must navigate without sufficient advising or oversight from older people. Even when their older family members or more seasoned colleagues seek to provide guidance, they do so in a virtual world they don't have to navigate themselves. Today, people must develop and execute a certain level of savvy to navigate these digital spaces as well as the organic interpersonal spaces where social capital is formed.

For first-generation college graduates, success is not simply about earning a degree; it is about decoding, navigating, and surviving systems never designed with their flourishing in mind.

The "hidden curriculum", comprised of the unspoken norms around networking, opportunity, and advancement, is often invisible until its absence becomes glaring (Chhajer, Chaudhry, & Mishra, 2024; Calderon Leon et al., 2024).

Malla Haridat reflected on this realization:

> *"I thought the reason I went to Columbia was for the education, the grades, the degree. But it was really about the social capital."*

Her degree, while valuable, was not the full currency of success.

The ideal web of relationships, mentorship, and access that others seemed to inherit effortlessly remained elusive.

Graduates entering professional worlds without this social roadmap often find themselves navigating elite spaces while carrying the internal weight of isolation.

They may be present, credentialed, and celebrated, yet still feel profoundly disconnected.

The emotional labor of translation—learning unspoken rules, decoding coded language, managing visibility and invisibility—becomes a second, invisible curriculum that few acknowledge but many endure.

Lonely Graduation in Leadership

As I stated earlier in the book, each contributor was asked a series of questions during my interviews. The opening question each time was: "What does lonely graduation mean to you?" As we explored lonely graduation in the context of leadership, Kevan Turman shared his robust response:

> *"I think when you think about leadership, there's this dichotomy of two different worlds. It's the world that people see, right? The big office—you've made it. You know, the accolades, the titles, the salary, the car, all the things that are sexy. But then, when I say the dichotomy of two worlds, it's the world that manages a team of seventeen, and I sometimes want to vent and have a safe space, and want someone to care about me. Like if the team comes in and they all have food, right, or they're chopping it up at the water cooler.*

Further examining the weight of leadership, Kevan adds:

> *You know, there are things leaders will probably never vocalize: an innate feeling of wanting to be included, only to realize that same title excludes you."*

Kevan described leadership as a split reality, a life lived in two worlds. Everyone recognizes the first world: the corner office, the title, the salary, the prestige, the visible signs that say *you made it*. That world is celebrated and admired.

But there's another world leaders occupy, one far quieter and rarely acknowledged. It is the world where you're responsible for a team you cannot fully confide in, where you want room to vent or to simply be cared for without the burden of being attached to your role and its expectations. It's the feeling of watching your team laugh together over lunch or swap stories casually in the hallway, and knowing that, no matter how warm the dynamic might be, your title still places you on the outside of the circle. Leaders rarely admit this loneliness out loud, but they feel the desire to belong colliding with the reality that leadership separates you from the very community you're trying to serve.

Academic graduations can be isolating, but so, too, can leadership.

As individuals ascend in professional, academic, or social hierarchies, the emotional terrain often becomes lonelier.

The weight of responsibility grows heavier as the circle of relatable peers narrows.

Elevation, while celebrated, often comes at the cost of proximity, emotional, cultural, and relational, to the communities that once anchored individuals.

Leadership, particularly for those breaking racial, gender, or first-generation barriers, frequently requires navigating spaces without models, without maps, and often without meaningful emotional support.

It is a complex loneliness, the honor of being in leadership coupled with the burden of being alone.

As Jin and Ikeda (2024) and Nichols and McBride (2017) found, leadership loneliness is an emotional experience that can have long-term impacts on psychological well-being, decision-making, and self-perception if not actively addressed.

Thus, graduating into leadership marks professional advancement in tandem with entering a new, often lonelier chapter of one's emotional journey.

Kevan goes on to offer insights on the connection to graduation:

> *"So when I look at graduation, it's not just graduating from high school, college, or a master's or doctorate or any terminal degree. I look*

at graduation, or, as you know, deeper than just, I'm looking at it as any elevation, like graduating out of, you know, the hood you may have come from or graduating out of, you know, you know, being religious and focusing more on relationship, like there's, there's all these elevations of life and but when you when you know better, you do better. And sometimes that is really, really lonely, because now you see it for what it is. And you had this beautiful lived experience with tons of like, messy middle moments right where now you're at a place where you take full agency over your life and your career and how you truly show up in the world. And so that epiphany is your epiphany. And so now here you are, at said level. It could be whatever, and that, to me, is when it's probably a lot from just your one response or one question, but in my opinion, like I'm triggered because that's lonely and it's it's hard to to to articulate that, particularly because Most people aren't going to hold space, because even if I complain about my lonely, they're looking at that as a problem that they would love to have, because my lonely is attached to all these things that look good, but they don't realize the hell that you have to actually go through, or the moments where you just really want to be a sound bar without looking like You're weak or you're, you know, all the things and so for me, that that dichotomy of Two Worlds is like, I would love to create a space where all things can be true, but, you know, I feel like sometimes you graduate into a position where you're losing direct connection with people, places and things, because you have to make such hard decisions."

Kevan's reflection pushes us to see graduation not as a moment, but as a migration. It is a movement into a new level of responsibility, consciousness, and agency. And like any migration, it requires leaving something behind. Whether that departure is geographic, cultural, spiritual, or professional, what is left unsaid in most public celebrations of success is that elevation requires separation. You are gaining clarity, but you are also shedding closeness. You are expanding, but you are also unmooring.

That is the quiet truth of *Lonely Graduation*: we celebrate the outcome, yet rarely acknowledge the emotional exit. We honor the accomplishment, but not the distance it creates. We applaud the leader's authority, but not their forfeiture of the shared vulnerability that leadership demands. As Kevan pointed out, many people admire the view from the mountaintop without realizing how few people can stand there with you once you arrive.

This loneliness is particularly sharp for leaders who are the first in their families, communities, industries, or identities to ascend. Their elevation disrupts expectations. It reorders relationships. It breaks inherited scripts. And because they are charting a path without a precedent, there is no inherited empathy waiting for them, no collective memory to soften the journey. The celebration of their success often obscures the cost of their transformation.

Lonely Graduation, then, is not about the absence of achievement, but rather the emotional labor that achievement carries with it. It asks us to name the costs that come with agency, the isolation that accompanies awakening, and the identity that is reshaped by responsibility. Kevan helps us see that leadership is about what one gains as much as what one must release: proximity, simplicity, and the assumption of belonging. To lead, one must step into rooms where one is needed but not fully known. To graduate, one must walk across thresholds that few will understand, even as they applaud.

And that is the work this book seeks to illuminate, not the finish line, but the distance from completion to arriving at one's more integrated/fully realized self afterward. Not the applause, but the echo that remains long after the crowd has moved on.

Kevan's story helps us observe the context of loneliness in leadership. I, too, have felt that same void at various points in my journey. In fact, loneliness in leadership comes in many forms. For example, I recall a time when I left a team I was thrilled to be part of. I was a leader among those colleagues, and I had to transition to a different role with another organization. I found myself isolated, spending lunch alone, and not because my new team wasn't willing to connect; in fact, they were actually reaching toward me to build that connection in those relationships, but I was mourning the loss of my previous team and all of those moments and good times that we shared. My former squad was remarkably diverse, and being part of a team full of people who looked like me, with similar generational backgrounds and racial identities, allowed me to experience a sense I didn't in most other spaces. As you venture from culturally affirming places during your leadership journey, you may lose elements of safety and security as you pivot to and through different opportunities. So the loneliness I felt during that transition wasn't due to my inability to access a door to safety, connection, or openness. My loneliness stemmed from losing a level of cultural connection and affirmation that I valued, and I knew it would take work to expand my capacity to cultivate another space of cultural safety, even though I was the leader. Finding a place where I don't have to carry artistic and racial battle fatigue as a leader is essential because, as I've said before, your title sometimes renders your other social identifiers invisible. People do not give you the benefit of the doubt.

Transitions in leadership don't just relocate our bodies; they uproot our belonging. We often pretend that moving into a new role is simply an external shift: new office, new responsibilities, new colleagues. But what we rarely acknowledge is the inner work required to rebuild the cultural and emotional ecosystems that once made us feel whole. I wasn't missing a job; I was missing a shared language of experience. I was missing the ease of being understood without translation.

This is a form of lonely graduation. We celebrate elevation without preparing leaders for the displacement that comes with it. Joining a new team is to begin again, socially, culturally, and psychologically. You don't just need to learn the workflow; you must know the unspoken norms, the humor, the trust cues, the emotional safety routes, and the spaces where your identity will be affirmed rather than merely tolerated. Leadership asks us to build these pathways ourselves, often before we have even found comfort.

And herein lies the complexity: even when community is possible, it may not feel available. My new colleagues were open, warm, and willing. The loneliness I felt wasn't evidence of exclusion; it was evidence of loss. When you have worked in a space that mirrors your story, your cadence, and your culture, stepping into a new environment requires you to grieve the loss of the familiarity that once held you. It takes energy to translate yourself again. It takes vulnerability to trust again. And it takes time to feel free again.

This is why leaders of color often describe battle fatigue even in environments that are not outwardly hostile. The fatigue is not always about the harm we encounter; sometimes it is about the work required to exist. When you carry a title, people assume that power shields you from racial, cultural, or generational friction. But a title does not make you emotionally invincible or professionally immune to your social reality. Still, leadership can make your needs less visible. It can render your identity secondary, as if the role has consumed everything else you are or could be.

Ify captures the essence of this push/pull with belonging as leaders:

> *"I don't know if I'm too jaded or if I'm just further along from an early executive. I think lonely graduation can sometimes yield a desire to participate in inclusion. That's not always healthy... it's the part that we don't talk about... Well, if you're going through a lonely graduation, what are you willing to do to not be lonely? And I think you have to ask yourself questions about the surrounding environment, people who would be disrupted in your day to day? What are the things that are outside of your control and you would have to do to not have that feeling? Are those things that you can keep up and maintain and sustain? And then the other part is like, have you really graduated? You know, like, what then was your definition of graduation? And is it okay that you're lonely because you're still in route and not necessarily at a destination?"*

Lonely graduation, then, is the emotional gap between where we once belonged and where we are expected to lead. It's being in the space between those who understood us effortlessly and those who must learn to understand us over time. Leadership may change our position, but it does not erase our need for affirmation, safety, or community. Growth doesn't always feel like a gain. Sometimes, it first feels like an absence. And that absence is part of the journey we rarely talk about, though we quietly carry it.

Summary

The emotional complexity of transition reveals that success and loneliness are not opposites; they are frequent companions.

Graduation, leadership, and personal elevation offer opportunities for growth and celebration, but they also demand new emotional skills: the ability to reflect deeply, to navigate hidden systems without inherited maps, and to redefine fulfillment amid shifting landscapes of belonging.

Lonely Graduation gives language to this invisible labor, the emotional work that undergirds transformation but is rarely acknowledged, honored, or supported.

True resilience lies not just in achieving milestones, but in surviving and thriving through the turbulent, unseen emotional currents that accompany them.

PART III
FINDING MEANING
IN THE SILENCE

Graduation, career transitions, and leadership milestones often come with a surprising aftermath: a profound and unfamiliar stillness.

After years, sometimes decades, of chasing goals, external validation, and public achievement, many high achievers find themselves adrift in a rare and unsettling quiet.

Yet research shows it is precisely in these transitional pauses, these seasons of stillness, that the most profound emotional recalibration and personal transformation occur (Pang, 2022; Calderon Leon et al., 2024).

Stillness is not a void. It is an opportunity: to reflect, to redefine success, and to reclaim identity on one's own terms.

The Asset of Stillness

For those conditioned to constant movement, stillness can feel unnatural, even threatening.

Studies affirm that high achievers often conflate busyness with self-worth, interpreting pauses as signs of failure, irrelevance, or weakness (Patel, Stentz, & Cougle, 2024; Wang et al., 2024).

However, it is in the moments of intentional pause that clarity, purpose, and deeper meaning emerge.

These simple, radical acts of stillness challenge internalized narratives that equate constant striving with value.

Psychological research shows that engaging in reflective practices during life and stage-of-life transitions strengthens emotional resilience, enabling individuals, especially those from marginalized backgrounds, to create internal anchors that outlast external applause (Chhajer, Chaudhry, & Mishra, 2024).

Stillness is not stagnation. It is an intentional reclamation of time, emotion, and agency.

Those of you who know me personally know that I am a cigar aficionado and enjoy regularly taking the time to sit still and puff a cigar. Now I'm not advocating for everyone to take up smoking cigars, but I recall a time when I watched a clip of Steve Harvey discussing why he loves smoking cigars. He considers it a form of yoga. He works demanding hours and spends considerable time on the go, so when he has a chance to sit still with a cigar, he gets a moment to sit and reflect on his breathing and just take a minute to be still. His words resonate with me as I consider this concept of stillness. For many of us, we have to discover where our moments are to actually just sit and focus on being at peace without movement. Meditation, prayer, and other activities can generate this pause. Still, as a cigar smoker, I've learned to look forward to it as a moment to ground myself regularly, so it has been helpful for me as a practice. Another valuable element to practice is being patient and sitting with stillness during meetings; I do not fill gaps of silence as a leader and do not rush to solve problems. Instead, I take in the context of what's going on and observe the room's (or Zoom's) energy and colleagues' intentions. I just let them exist without trying to edit any of the moments to soothe my own impatience.

The ability to bridge stillness and reflection fosters an awareness that supports overall well-being.

For much of life, success is measured through visible milestones: degrees earned, promotions won, accolades secured.

But true, sustainable success often emerges through less visible but more enduring victories: self-awareness, inner peace, and sovereignty over one's identity (Sease et al., 2024).

Stillness forces essential questions:

- What am I truly chasing?
- Whose approval have I been seeking?
- What does success mean to me, on my own terms?

Research shows that practicing reflection during significant life transitions guards against loneliness, depression, and identity fragmentation (Wang et al., 2024).

Individuals who root themselves in internal measures of success move through uncertainty with greater emotional agility than those grounded in external applause.

From the University of Oxford's Sheldonian Theatre, Kathleen remembers the quiet morning when she sensed the shift in acknowledgement within herself upon graduating with her doctorate. While raising two small children, she completed a challenging dissertation and believed she could now handle anything, no longer relying on external validation. Kathleen Lawton-Trask encapsulated this internal shift:

> *"Real becoming doesn't happen under the spotlight. It happens in the quiet, where no one's watching."*

Reflection is not indulgence; it is survival for those seeking to thrive beyond performative success.

Falling in Love with the Process

So much of modern ambition is fixated on "the moment", the graduation, the title, the salary threshold.

But real fulfillment does not arrive fully formed in a single, spectacular instance.

It grows through devotion to the ongoing, imperfect process of becoming.

Devin Johnson emphasized the critical shift:

> *"If you fall in love with the process, the ups and downs won't take you out."*

This mindset reflects what Yosso (2005) describes as aspirational capital, the ability to maintain hope and momentum despite external obstacles.

Such a perspective also aligns with findings that process-oriented thinking builds resilience to withstand the inevitable fluctuations of achievement and recognition (Chhajer, Chaudhry, & Mishra, 2024).

Success, then, is not a prize to be won, but a path to be walked.

As a school leader, I'm all about the process. There are specific actions I take at the start of every school year that are tried, accurate, and predictable. They are essential in setting expectations and maintaining a rhythm for the school year. For example, I always begin my initial meetings with faculty and staff by sharing statistical information we've gathered from our annual surveys, 360 reviews, and other data collection. This allows them to understand the resources that I've used to help decode the essence of what our school community wants us to focus on. This also positions me to demonstrate transparency as a leader while obtaining buy-in for implementations we will apply. Presenting the data is a point on a long road; it involves administering the survey tools, synthesizing the resulting data, and distilling it into a series of talking points and slides that affirm what our community is asking for while also being enlightening. It is a process.

Some people assume leadership is getting up in front of people, delegating tasks, and telling people what to do, but it's much more than that. And sometimes it's none of that. Leadership is the ability to hold vast amounts of (often sensitive) information and to know when to filter out the correct information at the right pace for the right impact. Being impulsive and only seeking the instant gratification of applause will not allow you to lead successfully. It will not allow you to be an exceptional steward of your own career. You must care a great deal about what you're doing to fall in love with the process of executing it. You don't get that way overnight. It's not an easy task to absorb into a habit, but once it's a part of your psychology, it is magical.

Why Success is a Moving Goalpost

The moment one milestone is reached, another looms on the horizon.

Graduates quickly realize that success is not a static destination. It's a target in perpetual motion.

Devin Johnson was candid in his reflection:

> *"In corporate terms, success just means you're responsible for achieving more success. If you hit a goal, the goalpost moves. There's always the next thing."*

This phenomenon is not merely psychological; it is structural.

As Nie, Chen, and Yu (2023) argue, systems of labor and achievement are designed to perpetuate endless striving, particularly for marginalized groups who must continually prove their worth.

Understanding this reality through the lens of communal cultural wealth reminds us that aspirational, navigational, and resistant capital, not just institutional validation, are vital for emotional survival and systemic disruption (Yosso, 2005).

As a K-12 administrator, I see the egoal post constantly swaying in the distance. Calls for innovation in one season and in the next wave in education are the "shiny objects" that articles, journals, and conferences tend to highlight. Additionally, according to several Black male educators I know, there's a tug of war going on to get talented Black male educators out of the classroom and into these administrative seats. The beauty of being a classroom teacher is that each school year, you get to reinvent and find new ways to engage with students. In the classroom, the focal point is to help develop the students in front of you every day. It's an unambiguous directive. That's very healthy, and that's why teachers can thrive across the longevity of their careers. Many teachers who move into the administrative space struggle because the goalposts are always moving: more results, more assessments, more measurables, more metrics, more ways to determine what must be known, applied, and quantified. How are we doing? What are we doing? And the reward for achieving goals and objectives is just another milestone to surpass more effectively the following year.

Holistically, we should be thriving if our students are thriving. Yes, we need ways to measure growth and academic progression. Success can become an expected outcome, while its pressures can grow heavier and become another responsibility to navigate.

Prepare yourself to know that you get an opportunity to hit a goal. Enjoy for a moment, but just know that there's another one. There's another peak, there's another hill to climb.

The Power of Strategic Positioning

Opportunity, contrary to popular myth, is not distributed solely on the basis of merit.

It hinges on visibility, credibility, timing, and access to networks of influence, forms of social and navigational capital that are critical for sustained success (Yosso, 2005).

Devin Johnson observed:

> *"When I tried to raise money at 42, nobody was interested. Now, at 52, having scaled a business, I have credibility. Same person. Just ten years of experience makes all the difference."*

Access and opportunity compound over time, favoring those who understand and can patiently navigate the invisible architectures of power, such as reading the room, understanding power dynamics, and knowing when to ask a question during a conversation.

This understanding transforms the narrative from one of individual inadequacy to one of strategic empowerment.

In the early 2010s, I interviewed at USC for the Director of Global Education position. I had no idea how I would perform the required duties and found myself bombing in real time during the interview. You see, to be the director of global education, I had to have some sense of world events, cultures, and trends. I hadn't even traveled outside the country much at the time, and here I was trying to convey my strategic vision for bringing the university's international brand of education to the masses. Now I had the skills to be functional in the job, but my timing was off regarding the necessary live experience and cultural exposure. My visibility was off; I couldn't see how this interview was coming across. I did not have enough navigational capital to connect the dots and demonstrate that I was eager to learn and had transferable skills to offer in a way that would earn me the role. I had enough education and professional experience to garner the interview panel's interest, but I lacked overall self-awareness to understand what they actually saw in me. On paper, they recognized my ability to connect, engage, and build systems. Had I rested in my strengths and maximized the expression of how I could utilize them for this opportunity, I would've been fine. Instead, my inexperience didn't register that I was just unqualified. I needed more collaboration, more sponsorship, and more navigational awareness to convey that I, too, recognized why I was their ideal candidate. The good news is that experience served as an opportunity to learn from that situation. I realized other skills had to be a part of my toolkit if I wanted to be successful. Looking back on that experience, I was not the right fit. It wasn't the right job, and my passion wasn't there, but it was an opportunity for me to become much more strategic in my preparation for such opportunities.

The Politics of Graduation and Departure

During my interview sessions, I also tried to elicit participants' perspectives and to contemplate the experiences of figures in the public eye. Specifically, I asked each person for their thoughts on two historical figures during groundbreaking moments: 1) how Barack Obama hypothetically processed his thoughts as he drove away from the White House after transitioning power to Donald Trump, and 2) what was the lonely graduation experience for Kamala Harris after the night of the 2024 presidential election?

Graduation is often imagined as a freely chosen celebration, an earned moment of applause, an achievement recognized by all. But political graduation reveals another truth: sometimes departure is forced, muted, or rendered lonely by the very structures a person has transformed. As Ify Ike insightfully declared:

"Barack Obama... graduated into the class of former presidents."

In this framing, graduation isn't a walk across a stage; it is an assignment into a new identity category, whether one chooses it or not. It is a sorting process imposed by institutions, media, and public memory. It is an exile disguised as honor, where the transition is shaped less by personal accomplishment and more by what a community (in this case, an entire nation and larger world) is willing, or unwilling, to recognize.

It reflects a shift in identity, often without applause and sometimes amid active opposition (Dor-Haim, 2023).

Through resistant capital, which includes the knowledge and skills developed in response to opposition (Yosso, 2005), individuals redefine graduation not as abandonment but as evolution, moving toward being freer, more authentic versions of themselves.

Graduation Without the Game: Obama and the Constraints of Being First

Graduation for firsts, defined as the first person to break the barrier of marginalization, helped by a dominant group in a role or position, does not merely end a chapter; it ends access to the fight one entered and hoped to transform. Dennis Ellis, reflecting on Barack Obama's departure from his eight-year presidency, named a quiet sorrow beneath the spectacle of his exit:

> *"He probably left feeling he should have accomplished more... the job being the first didn't allow him to do that."*

To graduate as "the first" is to be denied the full range of possibilities others are granted. Dennis pushed this further when we talked, arguing that Obama faced a greater constraint than legendary Jackie Robinson:

> *"With Robinson, you're either going to hit the ball or you're not. But Obama didn't get to play the game he wanted to play."*

Being first means playing by rules not built for you, and then being evaluated against a game you were never allowed to fully participate in. As the first Black President, he carried the responsibility to honor the magnitude of being a "first" to such a degree that he could not operate with the full depth of his unique instincts. Obama's "graduation" into the class of former presidents was thus not only a ceremonial exit but also the forced conclusion of an unfinished pursuit of "hope."

Graduation, here, is not triumph. It is truncated potential, constrained by racial expectations, partisan obstruction, and the burden of symbolizing progress while being denied the tools to enact it.

Graduation and the Question of Legacy

For political graduates, legacy becomes a haunting question:

"What's the thing I'm going to be remembered for?"

Ellis wondered whether Obama's internal dialogue has ever and continues to wrestle with the limits imposed on him:

- Did he question if his primary legacy would be rescuing the country from a historic financial crisis?
- He may have pondered if his defining achievement was passing the Affordable Care Act.
- He wondered if his most significant contribution was successfully ending the hunt for Osama bin Laden.
- Alternatively, he might have feared that his memory would be overshadowed by the controversies that others weaponized against him.

Graduation whispers a question few dare to confront publicly: Is completion the same as fulfillment?

The Misrecognized Graduate: When Achievement Is Not Believed

If Barack Obama's graduation was marked by constraint, Kamala Harris's was and remains defined by misrecognition. Ify Ike called her transition into the "class of women who dared to run" a boundary placed around her achievement, a form of containment disguised as categorization.

Dennis Ellis expanded on this through lived proximity. He does not speak hypothetically. He says as someone who knows her:

"She had done everything right to get there, and she didn't get what she deserved."

Kamala's graduation is neither an ascent nor a loss. It is a rejection. Ellis names the wound stripped of political language:

"I think she thinks it was a rejection of her, which is terrible."

The pain of this is not that she lost; she has lost before. It is that she won in preparation, qualification, debate, and vision, yet was still not granted victory. She was the superior candidate.

> *This is the cruel paradox of political commencement: some graduates don't get the diploma even after completing the work.*

The Violence of Reverse Graduation

Ify calls this phenomenon "reverse graduation", the attempt to walk someone back into a status they have already transcended:

> *"They want to act like you didn't achieve the thing."*

Reverse graduation is a structural erasure. It does not deny the effort; it denies the achievement's legitimacy. It is not failure, it is disqualification after qualification. Ellis sees this clearly when he imagines the loneliness Kamala must sit with:

> *"She probably is having a lonely graduation."*

At this graduation, the applause was in recognition of a race well run. The quiet brutality of political departure is that some graduates must celebrate in isolation what a nation refuses to honor.

Graduation as Evolution, Not Acceptance

So what does graduation offer? In thinking about Harris, Ify notes that she now has perspective on her side from the election, which can provide dignity, self-recognition, even liberation:

> *"I've graduated into the class of free time... reflection... the class of 'Do I want to deal with these people again?'"*

Graduation, then, can be a movement not into new power, but into genuine autonomy. Resistant capital (Yosso, 2005) becomes the tool through which uncelebrated graduates author their next chapter. Political graduates must create their own ceremonies because institutional ceremonies will not celebrate them when they are not the victor, and sometimes even when they are.

The celebration is not public. It is internal. It is not shared. It is sovereign.

Kathleen Lawton-Trask spoke to internal transformations that occur even as the external world celebrates visible wins:

> *You don't become president or vice president and stay the same. You evolve in public, and often you evolve alone.*

She pointed out that the real graduation for leaders like Obama and Harris is not from job title to job title; it is from one iteration of self to another, in full view of a world that often prefers simple narratives over messy, human ones.

What Comes After the Uncelebrated Walk?

Graduation in political life is not a procession of joy. It is often a solitary walk into a new identity, shaped not by applause but by misrecognition, obstruction, constrained possibility, or outright rejection.

Something powerful resides in that quiet walk: the graduate's authority over their own narrative. Obama does not need to return to politics to prove his legacy. Harris does not need public affirmation to validate his qualification. Their graduation is not an end but an evolution, a transition into spaces where they can finally choose themselves.

They may not have been celebrated as they should have been, but they did not leave empty-handed. They left knowing the truth of what they offered, and knowing something the institution could not imagine:

They will not return to the class they surpassed. Even if Harris runs again, the first attempt still happened, and it was important.

It is a complicated, often isolating evolution.

Obama and Harris remind us that reaching success at the highest levels does not erase loneliness; it transforms it.

Lonely graduation is not an anomaly.

It is the unseen, sacred cost of becoming more visible in structures that were never built for your full humanity.

And yet, in their journeys, and in the reflections of those who watch and walk similar paths, there is also a quiet hope: *that visibility, no matter how lonely, still plants seeds.*

It still cracks ceilings.

It still opens doors.

In honoring the loneliness behind visible success, we acknowledge the fullness of the story, not just its headlines.

The DEI Reckoning as
a Forced Graduation

Let's take the context of graduation into the conversation around social justice and equity work. Before 2020's social justice reckoning, many justice workers and equity practitioners experienced the nuances of the lack of closure that comes when a potential path toward liberation meets opposition. This dynamic is the cause of its own book.

The national backlash against Diversity, Equity, and Inclusion (DEI) is not a mere political shift; it is a form of forced graduation. The receding waters of change back to dangerous ideologies of oppression ushered justice-centered practitioners into a new chapter, not by readiness, but by the braided line of oppression (interpersonal, ideological, and institutional). Oppression functions the way some graduations do: the institution decides the ceremony is over, even when the work is unfinished.

Ify Ike reflected on this disillusionment with clarity and conviction:

> *"The real DEI folks aren't lamenting this moment the same way, because we were doing justice work before we called it DEI."*

In other words, DEI was never the work; liberation was.

It was merely the acronym for a labor that long predated PowerPoint frameworks, titles, and institutional branding campaigns.

This is where our resistant capital, which fosters the skills needed to challenge inequity through opposition, emerges and is in motion. Yosso (2005) describes this form of capital as the knowledge, skills, and strategies that marginalized communities cultivate to navigate and transform oppressive structures. DEI as a field may be forced to contract, but justice work as a cultural inheritance does not. Its legitimacy is not determined by market favorability.

Still, forced graduations always take something from us.

They require us to step into a new "class" of practitioners, one in which the safety of institutional endorsement is gone, the metrics have shifted, and the public appetite is unpredictable. As Ify described in other points of our conversation, transitions that occur under exceptional pressure can fracture identity. They can make us question whether we still belong, or whether our labor—and thus our contributions and identity—has been erased, reversed, or suddenly deemed unnecessary.

Yet, in this reframed landscape, something essential becomes visible.

DEI was a temporary home; equity work is a permanent lineage.

If DEI roles are disappearing, the people who built that field are not.

If institutions are retreating, communities are not.

And in that recognition lies the more profound truth: this is not a sunset; it's a sorting. A moment that reveals who was doing the work because it was structurally incentivized and who was doing the job because it was spiritually non-negotiable.

Justice workers are not mourning their identity. They are mourning the broken agreement of solidarity and restoration that it seemed like the nation was ready for. They are graduating into a new phase of the struggle, one where their authority comes not from job titles but from lived experience, historical continuity, and communal memory.

The moral horizon that DEI attempted to formalize remains. Those who were anchored in legacy will continue to move forward, carried by the same communities that sustained it long before institutions had language for it.

This forced graduation is not gentle. But it is clarifying.

PART IV

THE CALL TO ACTION

Graduation, whether from school, a career, a leadership role, or an identity, does not mark an ending.

It is merely a transformation, a shift into the next, often undefined, stage of becoming.

The challenge is no longer achieving success for its own sake, but instead learning how to utilize it best once it has been attained.

As research on life transitions suggests, the real work of growth often begins after the milestone, when we must decide how to share wisdom, uplift others, and find meaning beyond the confines of individual achievement (Calderon Leon et al., 2024; Wang et al., 2024).

This final stage of the journey calls us not just to reflect, but also to act.

To ensure that our experiences, our struggles, and our victories become fuel for the flourishing of others.

The Final Graduation: Giving It All Away

At some point, every leader, entrepreneur, and changemaker must confront a critical question:

What legacy am I leaving?

Actual graduation is measured by how much wisdom we pour into the world beyond ourselves.

To Bryant, success is not about hoarding knowledge, titles, or power.

It is about giving everything away through mentoring, teaching, and creating pathways for others to journey farther, faster, and with less suffering. One of the ways I give back comes in the way of my podcast "On the Way to School", where I share stories and offer examples of how I try to lead in my school.

Yet too often, knowledge is hoarded instead of shared, perpetuating cycles of isolation and struggle that could be dismantled through communal generosity (Yosso, 2005; Sease et al., 2024).

Transitions terrify those who cling to power.

The reluctance to graduate, to move on, and to evolve often stems from fear of irrelevance rather than from a lack of opportunity.

Ify Ike articulated this systemic dysfunction:

> *"We have what we have in politics because these motherfuckers are hoarders."*

Leadership should be about stewardship: building spaces where others can rise.

Instead, hoarded power undermines the familial and social capital needed to sustain vibrant, just communities (Yosso, 2005).

Authentic leadership recognizes that real success lies in collective ascent, not personal preservation to the perpetual detriment of others.

Community Cultural Wealth is a framework that teaches us how true wealth is measured by what we collectively build and distribute rather than our personal accumulation (Yosso, 2005).

Familial, social, and resistant capital thrive when wisdom is treated as an abundant resource with communal inheritance.

I recall deciding to leave Scripps College in Claremont, CA, to work at the Collegiate School in New York City. I was a dean and loved my Scripps team, but understood that my ascent there had been swift, and that several other rockstars would benefit from my getting out of their way! The option to transition arrived before I was mentally ready to start a new journey, but the unfolding NYC opportunity was only open for a short window. You see, I went to NYC in 2018, and we all know what happened in 2020, the COVID-19 pandemic. Choosing to sit on success and hoard the authority I had accumulated in partnership at Scripps would've prevented the growth I found in the next collaboration at Collegiate. The transition to NYC allowed me to live in Manhattan and do deep equity work at one of the country's oldest schools. Both jobs stretched me in ways that I didn't know existed and made me a better person. Choosing comfort and staying in Claremont would've meant missing out on something that ultimately added skills and memories to my life.

The Responsibility of Sharing What We've Learned

Many of us were taught that success is an individual pursuit.

But nearly none of us arrive at its shores alone.

Could every opportunity, every lesson, every breakthrough be shaped, directly or indirectly, by someone else's influence, generosity, or sacrifice?

The real question is: Are we paying that forward?

Are we:

Mentoring the next generation?

- Demystifying the hidden pathways to leadership for those not tracked to travel them?
- Making the journey less lonely for others?

Dennis Ellis reflected on the tension between isolation and responsibility:

> *"There's no manual for this [leadership]. But just because there's no manual doesn't mean we shouldn't leave notes for the ones coming behind us."*

True success demands that we turn inward reflections into outward impact (Bruss, Seth, & Zhao, 2024; Yosso, 2005).

That's why I wrote this book. I have a responsibility to contribute to the body of available knowledge on personal development and spiritual evolution, so others can learn from and grow. Dennis is right. There is no manual for the growth and impact of life after achieving significant milestones, but as we look back with more focus, one can be distinguished.

While not a manual, this book can help us step into the guidance uniquely tailored to each of us. Mine doesn't look like yours, and yours doesn't look like mine, but there are similarities. When we share our experiences, we can then find community on our collective paths.

The Role of Mentorship and Community in Breaking the Cycle

A lonely graduation is not a personal failure.

It is a systemic phenomenon, repeated across industries, generations, and communities.

One of the most potent ways to disrupt this cycle is through intentional mentorship and community-building.

Mentorship is not about prescribing answers.

It is the act of walking beside someone as they find their own solutions.

It requires creating spaces where vulnerability, uncertainty, and aspiration are welcomed rather than judged.

As Ify Ike shared:

> *"We don't need to hoard wisdom the way institutions hoard power. We need to spread it like seeds."*

Research confirms that mentorship and community ties are critical in buffering loneliness, fostering resilience, and building sustainable success networks (Sease et al., 2024; Patel, Stentz, & Cougle, 2024).

When we invest in others' journeys, we turn lonely graduations into communal celebrations of becoming.

I recall making it to St. Paul, Minnesota, in 2002. I've already told you about Dr. Chatman, the most impactful mentor in my life, but during that same season, I met another person who made a significant impact on who I was becoming. Mentors don't always have a formal title or tenure. This person arrived as a friend I met through a teammate from St. Paul, but the wisdom he shared helped me understand the moment in my life I was entering. Cory Vaughn was my narrator for life in the Twin Cities. He made it his job to introduce the cities to anyone from California on behalf of the state, because he had great pride in representing his home. So there we were on some night in January 2002, riding in his Dodge Intrepid, heading down 94W. He was explaining the capital city of St. Paul, its traditions, and Minneapolis's industry. Almost on cue, we came down the highway and the Metrodome, out of nowhere, popped up in the skyline, complemented by skyscrapers. I mean, it was cinematic! My first lesson was his tour of the city, which expanded my understanding of the opportunities to be a part of this collective space. What began as a tour was really a moment to reflect on the significance of the community I was immersed in. It gave me a sense of pride in where I now stood as a newcomer. Subsequent lessons included how to find a light in the nightclub, stand under it, and smile so everyone could see you, thus making you stand out in the crowd and have an impact on the nightclub scene. That is a lesson that I have since passed on to my children, but I digress. Cory also became my barber after I graduated. I sat in his chair every Tuesday on my lunch break when I began working. He was proud of his city and remained a supportive, open book to ensure others would succeed in his hometown. I appreciate him for those times, and I know he continues to do the same for so many others.

Cory's impact provided a level of orientation to my new home. In many ways, colleges and universities create similar programming for new students. In some instances, those programs do a great job of bridging the gap between high school graduation and the first year of college. Companies do the same thing when they pair new hires with mentors or buddies during their first 90 days or first year. To break the cycle of loneliness, feel free to seek out mentorship and other ways to orient and connect during your moment of transition.

Success as a Journey, Not a Destination

One of the most challenging but most liberating realizations after significant achievements is that there is no final arrival.

Success is dynamic, ever-evolving, and deeply personal.

Malla Haridat revealed:

> *"There's no 'made it.' There's just the next door you open, and the next room you build."*

We are taught to chase and cross finish lines.

Sustainable achievement lies in embracing success as an ongoing, lifelong evolution, redefining goals, re-centering purpose, and allowing identity to transform as needed.

Growth is not linear.

It is cyclical, layered, and deeply human.

The best leaders and visionaries are not those who cling to past titles.

They are those who remain curious, open, and courageous enough to reinvent themselves again and again.

Kathleen Lawton-Trask offered:

> *"The applause ends. The curtain falls. And then, if you're brave, you start creating without needing an audience."*

Lonely Graduation centers on naming becoming as a perpetual state. It is not a crisis, though it often presents as one, but a calling.

Those who survive major life transitions ask better, braver questions of themselves rather than pretending to know all the answers or seeking to know them all.

Resilience is built through and within willingness to evolve, even and especially when the world expects you to remain the same.

The most profound way to give meaning to our own lonely transitions is to walk others through theirs.

If we have known what it feels like to reach a summit and find it strangely empty, we have the requisite wisdom to guide others or help them guide themselves through their climbs.

Adequate support of others requires:

- **Listening without judgment.**
- **Sharing without condescension.**
- **Encouraging without overshadowing.**

Malla Haridat put it plainly:

> *"Sometimes the best thing you can do is sit with someone in their confusion. Not solve it. Just sit."*

By doing so, we transform lonely graduations from cycles of isolation into cycles of empowerment and hope.

Reflection is also critical.

But without action, reflection risks becoming inertia.

The final stage of any actual transition is moving forward with intention:

- Mentoring others navigating lonely transitions
- Building communities where vulnerability is honored, not punished
- Challenging systems that perpetuate isolation at the highest levels

🦅 Creating opportunities rooted in resilience, inclusion, and belonging

Drawing on Community Cultural Wealth, we realize that our aspirational, navigational, social, linguistic, familial, and resistant capitals are not private possessions. I've recognized this as people remind me about how my presence impacts them as I navigate the space as a school leader. I don't always have time to talk to the younger Black professionals, but they often share with me, in passing, that my navigational impact helps them navigate the professional atmosphere as well.

They are communal gifts we are called to multiply (Yosso, 2005).

We didn't come this far just to crown ourselves. We came this far to build bridges.

Summary

Graduation is a calling to become bigger than our milestones, louder than our applause, and more generous than our perceived opportunities.

I hope *Lonely Graduation* reminds you that becoming never stops.

It demands reflection, yes.

It demands action even more.

In answering that call, we transform lonely transitions into launching points for ourselves and for all those yet to come.

The journey does not end here.

It never does.

Embracing the Silence,
Reframing the Story

The moments of silence, transition, and uncertainty that emerge after milestones are not voids.

They are thresholds, distinctive invitations:

- To reflect.
- To redefine.
- To create something entirely new.

They are when and where we decide to be the architects of a story that is deeper, truer, and freer, rather than survivors of our success.

Once we have achieved, once we have crossed the stage, once we have "arrived."

What comes next?

That answer belongs to us.

Inherited definitions of success do not bind us.

We are not obligated to chase milestones that no longer nourish our spirit.

We have the right, and the responsibility, to define success on our own terms, shaped by our dreams, our communities, and the wisdom forged in every lonely graduation we have endured.

Our journey is not about arriving at a final destination.

It is about owning the next chapter, fully, courageously, and intentionally.

Loneliness is not only a wound.

It can be a wellspring of self-discovery, growth, and radical clarity.

The key is not to fear the silence.

Listen to what the silence asks of us:

- What do I need?
- What do I truly want?
- Who am I becoming?
- How can my experience be a gift to others?

In answering these questions, we do not eliminate loneliness.

We transform it into intention, into sovereignty, and into the architecture of a new kind of success.

It is within the silence, not beyond it, that we reclaim our agency.

Graduation, of any kind, fosters a deeper becoming.

The goal is not simply to achieve and move on.

It is to become the kind of person who:

- Finds meaning beyond milestones.
- Carries wisdom forward.
- Builds intentional community.
- Life's growth is an act of leadership and love.

The real question is not:

"What have we achieved?"

It is:

"What will we do with it?"

Our lonely graduations are not dressed-up failures.

They are sacred crossings, moments where we begin to embody the selves we were always meant to be

LETTERS TO THE LONELY GRADUATE

Everyone who has achieved a milestone, graduation, promotion, or new beginnings, knows the silence that follows after the applause fades.

Identity trembles, hope flickers, and loneliness often takes root.

When asked what they would say to someone standing in that silence, to someone facing their own lonely graduation season, those interviewed for *Lonely Graduation* answered with clarity. They would not offer platitudes to the recently accomplished and adrift. They would share profound, hard-earned truths with fellow life travelers. They have done so via the quotes I shared with you, dear reader.

Their words form a kind of collective letter: an offering to anyone finding themselves in the complicated, tender space after achievement.

Feel Everything, Without Shame

Emille Bryant would begin by telling you: Feel it all.

> *"Don't run from the loneliness. Don't rush to cover it up. Own it. Process it."*

Emille understands that high achievers are often taught to power through discomfort.

But true evolution requires the opposite: slowing down, honoring emotions, and allowing yourself to be reshaped by the transition, not crushed by it.

> *"Processing gives you the ability to stay on course," he reminds us.*
> *"It's not about fixing it. It's about surviving it, emotionally whole."*

The silence after graduation is not punishment, though it can be brutal.

It is an invitation to grieve, celebrate, reflect, and reimagine, all at once.

Know that the Ache Is Normal

Dennis Ellis would tell you: The loneliness isn't proof you did something wrong. It is evidence that you did something extraordinary.

"If you're feeling lonely, it's because you outgrew something. Maybe a role. Maybe a relationship. Maybe even an old version of yourself."

Experiencing or inhabiting loneliness after success is not a flaw; it's an inevitable consequence of growth.

Dennis's journey taught him that loneliness signals an evolution of identity, a shedding that is painful and necessary.

"You didn't fail," he insists. "You graduated."

A Milestone Along the Journey

Devin Johnson would share an affirming reminder:

> *"Graduation is not a destination or a finish line...it's a milestone on a long rich path forward with twists and turns, ups and downs,...it's a journey that continues to ask more of you and you continue to get back a lot in return. Success isn't a destination on the journey but more of a positive relationship with the path..."*

Graduation does not conclude the race.

It starts a new chapter, one with higher expectations, deeper challenges, and more internal questions than ever before.

Success, Devin reminds us, must be redefined from the inside, or it will always leave you feeling unfinished, unfulfilled, and quietly aching for more.

Give Yourself Permission to Pause

Stillness is inherent to success.

The compulsion to immediately move onto the next thing, next job, next goal, next accolade, only deepens loneliness. It will not provide alleviation.

Stillness, reflection, and rest are not indulgences.

They are necessities for authentic growth.

I'd say you don't have to earn your right to sit still; you already earned it.

Honor What You Have Survived

Your worth is not found in your latest accomplishment.

It is found in your perseverance, your reflection, and your ability to keep evolving even when no one is clapping.

One of the best aspects of this project is remembering and learning from the past. Emille helped me immensely as my executive coach by revisiting the methods that had worked for me in the past, not as time management habits, but rituals or memories that would align with my core values and sense of purpose.

So you must honor what you survived, because your latest accomplishment isn't where you've actually built your perseverance. You began forging it when you envisioned or set out to make that first attempt to try something, to try anything. I remember, in the summer of 1996, as a high school freshman, walking to my first football practice in August with a gallon of water, not knowing what I was doing. But I kept telling myself that this was the beginning of an era. It wasn't the era I anticipated; I was not very good on the field. But that perseverance I was mentally building kept me evolving. Even without any guarantee that anyone would reward or celebrate me, I demonstrated to myself that I can make it. Had I not gone to that practice, had I not struggled through playing the sport, none of my family or friends would have reprimanded me. There were no stakes; the bar was on the floor. Yet, by the time I was done with high school, I had established myself as a student athlete and learned a skill that actually carried me to college, and the rest, as they say, was history. So don't be afraid to reflect on what got you there, the mentality of hope and pursuit, but make sure to delve much deeper than your last victory. Go back to the first one, go back to the early days, go back to the times when there was no evidence that your efforts would pay off. That's the blueprint, the roadmap. Celebrate the version of you who chooses to get started.

When we reflect honestly, we notice that success rarely begins with skill. It starts with a decision, often a quiet one made without applause, evidence, or clarity about what comes next. Many people assume that leadership is earned later in life, through awards, promotions, or public wins. But those moments only reveal what was forged much earlier. Leadership is shaped in solitude before it is recognized in community.

That early shaping often comes with instability, pressure, and circumstances that should have disqualified us long before anyone praised our potential. That is why the story below matters. It reminds us that the leadership journey is often filled with contradictory moments of brilliance intertwined with immaturity, favor paired with proximity to failure, and a kind of perseverance that has nothing to do with knowing what you're doing and everything to do with refusing to quit.

That's what Dennis remembered when I asked him about support during his own rise. He spoke about an opportunity he almost missed as an intern at the California State Assembly:

> *"I was on the front page of The LA Times... a story about this former Titan lineman going to tackle state legislature. And right after that article came out, I'm sitting in jail behind something I didn't even do. I almost lost the job before I ever got there. So when I finally made it to Sacramento, I just sat there thinking, how did I end up in the middle of all these people?"*

We rarely talk about this kind of transition because it doesn't fit the mythology of "clean" success. This is not the polished journey that makes its way into bios, résumés, or ceremonial speeches. It is a reminder that some leaders arrive through narrow escapes, undeserved grace, and the discipline to keep showing up even while weighted by behaviors, associations, and worldviews that could have undone them.

At that time and in that room, Dennis did not feel pride alone; he felt humility, awareness, and a recognition that he had been placed among people who did not yet understand the impact of his journey. This was not because he was unworthy. He was unfinished. Success wasn't validating who he had been; it was transforming who he would become.

When we honor the early versions of ourselves, we don't just celebrate the wins. We honor the mess, the near misses, and the unpolished decisions we survived. Those are the moments that teach us, not how to look successful, but how to carry success responsibly once it arrives.

So as you reflect on your own journey, don't just celebrate the moments when others finally noticed you. Honor the version of you who showed up when no one was watching. Honor the part of your story that almost cost you everything or offered you nothing in return. That is where leadership was born long before it was recognized.

Find Your People (Even If It's Hard)

Ify Ike would advise you to seek community with intention, not convenience.

> *"You need people who can sit with you when you're growing, and not make you shrink to stay comfortable."*

The loneliness of elevation is real, but isolation doesn't have to be permanent.

Find people who celebrate not just your titles but also, and especially, your transitions.

Locate and nurture relationships with people who understand that growth is messy, uncertain, and beautiful.

If you cannot find that community, Ify reminds you that you have the right to build it.

When I asked Malla what she would share with someone in their season of lonely graduation, Malla shared that establishing mentorships is also a key life priority. She highlights that you can

> *Find mentors in bizarre and strange places... If you're at an event, you click with somebody you know, follow them on LinkedIn, and talk with them. If there's a trade association... I would attend professional association events and talk to people. You're in college, they'll talk to you... You have that even if you're right out of school, they'll still talk to you like, Oh, I just graduated. They'll talk to you because you're not a threat at that point. So, I think building your mentorship networks is the key one.*

Mentors rarely appear like characters in a movie who appear or descend at just the right moment, perfect roadmap in hand. More often, they show up through casual conversation or proximity. They emerge because we introduce ourselves, ask a question, sit at a new table, or dare to follow up. The people who shape our lives don't always enter through grand doors. Sometimes they arrive through accidental alignment: the panelist you stayed late to thank, the person you met while volunteering, the colleague who noticed your potential before you did.

But what matters most is not just finding people who will advise you. Find people who see you, who do not need you to shrink. Seek those who can expand your capacity without exploiting your ambition. Vibe with folks who aren't threatened by your growth and don't require demonstrated perfection to invest in your future.

Leadership can feel lonely, but loneliness should not become your lifestyle. Elevating your life does not mean shedding every relationship or standing at the top unaccompanied. You are allowed to build as you rise. You are allowed to learn from those who have walked longer roads, made more mistakes, and navigated the hidden curriculum you are just discovering. And you are allowed to find some of your greatest allies at unexpected moments.

Finding your people is not simply about collecting contacts; it is about creating a sense of belonging. You don't just gather mentors; you gather mirrors, people who help you see the fuller version of yourself. And when you find those mirrors, you don't just move forward alone. You move forward supported, seen, and strengthened.

Build Something that Is Yours

During seasons of transition, especially those marked by "lonely graduation," the ground beneath us can feel unstable. Systems that once rewarded our labor suddenly grow quiet. The identity that once defined us no longer fits. We become vulnerable to institutions that celebrate our performance, but not our humanity.

This is why Malla Haridat insists on ownership. Not theoretically. Not someday. Right now.

> *"The biggest one of all... you need to have ownership over your own career. A job is only always going to be a job."*

Having something that is yours, a business, creative work, a movement, a community practice, offers a stabilizing anchor when the world becomes unsteady. It becomes a refuge, a site of dignity, and a place where the whole self can exist without compromise. In seasons of transition, Malla stated, the work you've built with your own hands can save you.

> *"I've hit rock bottom a couple of times... and the thing that's always saved my soul...[was] my business."*

This held true when her mother became ill, and when she was caring for her daughter as a young parent.

What saved her was not a title, not a company, not a paycheck.

It was what she owned.

Ownership as Survival

Lonely graduations bring the jarring realization that you can ascend and still feel disposable. The world wants proof that you can show up, perform, and produce without guaranteeing belonging or recognition. As Christopher observed during their conversation:

> *"They want you to demonstrate that you can actually ascend here... versus just being able to show up and work."*

Systems demand performance. They rarely invest in permanence. If you collapse, they continue. If you succeed, the system will re-evaluate whether you were "supposed" to. If you are extraordinary, they often deny it.

Ownership resists disposability.

To own and retain something, such as a business or creative work, means you cannot be erased from your life's work. You cannot be walked back. You cannot be reverse-graduated.

Entrepreneurship as Resistant Capital

Malla's advice is neither romantic nor limited to people who already see themselves as founders. Her position is fundamentally about agency:

> *"Get you an entrepreneurship... with all the bad English I could possibly use right there."*

She is naming entrepreneurship as a mindset, not a career field, as resistant capital (Yosso, 2005). People who build for themselves develop networks, access, and room to maneuver beyond institutional permission.

> *"The connections you'll be able to make... the rooms you'll be able to get access to... people will see that spark within you."*

The spark is not the product. The spark is the agency.

Make Something Early; Before You Need It

Too many people wait to build something of their own, only to have a crisis force their hand. Malla sees this often as a coach:

> *"I work with a lot of folks that are waiting till our age (early forties), and I'm like, good lord, I don't think I could do that."*

Ownership developed late is triage.

Ownership developed early is the foundation.

She tells a simple, unglamorous story from her college years: collecting bottles after fraternity parties and recycling them for money. She did not pursue entrepreneurship as a status or branding. It was about learning the discipline of generating value independent of an institution.

> *"Create something for yourself that you have ownership over so that when you do hit that lonely point, there's still a thread... that keeps you going."*

Ownership is not an achievement. It is scaffolding.

Ownership and Emotional Well-Being

Building something of your own is not just a financial strategy; it should also serve as emotional protection. Malla situates entrepreneurship alongside therapy as a dual commitment to self-preservation:

> *"Get you some mental help."*

Malla felt that, for her generation (Gen X), journaling, prayer, or tarot cards were the best options available. Today, she advises recent college graduates and transitioning professionals to use every tool available: coaching, therapy, and community care.

> *"Commit to investing in your own mental and emotional help and support... and then do the work."*

Ownership without emotional support becomes burnout.
Emotional work without autonomy becomes dependence.
Lonely graduation requires both of you to move forward.

Conclusion: Build Before the Applause Stops

Build something that is yours before transition forces you to need it. Build before the applause fades, before the system shifts, before the institution decides who you are allowed to become.

Ownership does not prevent lonely graduation.

Ownership helps ensure that you survive it and grow from it.

When institutions fall silent, your work should not.

When titles shift, your identity should not collapse.

When roles end, your purpose should not lose oxygen.

As Malla stated:

> *"Take ownership over your own career... Superman is not coming to save us."*

So build.
Not later.
Now.

Build something that makes you undeniable, especially to yourself.

CONCLUSION
THE SACRED WORK
OF BECOMING

Lonely Graduation is not a failure.

It is sacred work.

It is the emotional terrain where real resilience, authenticity, and leadership are born.

It is the place where we stop measuring our worth by how loudly others cheer and start measuring it by how deeply we are willing to live our truth.

The journey after the milestone is often silent, solitary, and confusing.

But it is also rich, transformative, and powerful beyond measure.

If you are standing in that silence right now, know this:

You are not broken. You are becoming.

You are not abandoned.

You are being invited to build something more honest, more aligned, and more yours.

And somewhere, on another mountaintop or in another valley, someone else is walking through their lonely graduation too, carrying the same questions, the same heartaches and headaches, and the same stubborn, sacred hope.

You are not alone. You never were.

Bringing It All Together

This book is not just about the moment of graduation.

It is about what follows:

- Emotions we rarely discuss
- Realities of transition
- Ways we redefine success beyond traditional expectations

Lonely Graduation explores how success, solitude, and transformation intersect, and how we can navigate these moments with intention and grace.

For some, the transition beyond a milestone is exhilarating.

For others, it is disorienting, isolating, and filled with a haunting quiet.

I can remember the feeling plainly; nobody told me what either of my graduation days would feel like.

We are taught that achievement should deliver overwhelming joy.

But for many, the reality is far more complicated and far more human.

The Invitation to Redefine Success

At the heart of *Lonely Graduation* is the radical idea that loneliness is not always a deficit.

It is a **potential**, a hidden asset.

Solitude gives us space to:

- Reflect without performance
- Reframe inherited expectations
- Realign with what truly matters

It allows us to step outside the noise of external validation and ask ourselves anew:

- What does success mean to me now?
- Who am I beyond my achievements?
- What do I want to build next?

As Malla Haridat insisted:

"You need something that is yours. Something you own."

Ownership of our stories, our dreams, our futures, is the real graduation.

Leaving a Legacy

I hope *Lonely Graduation* imparts one lesson more than any others: it is this:

Success is not just about what we achieve.

It is about what we pass on.

Emille Bryant captured the spirit of this truth when he said:

> *"I want to die with an empty brain."*

We do not carry our experiences for ourselves alone.

We carry them to open doors for others.

To create better systems.

To leave behind wisdom that makes the journey lighter for those who come after us.

That is the truest graduation: the moment we stop climbing only for ourselves, and begin creating for the collective.y

Final Words

Wherever you are in your journey, whether standing at the threshold of a new milestone, navigating the silence after one, or preparing for another leap, know this:

You are not alone.

You never were.

And the next phase of your life, the one only you can define, is already waiting for you.

Walk toward it with courage.

Walk toward it with reflection.

Walk toward it with the fullness of everything you have carried and everything you have yet to become.

No lonely graduation is ever the end.

It is the beginning of your next, most honest becoming.

SUPPORTING SOMEONE THROUGH A LONELY GRADUATION

<u>**ROMANCE (Partners & Intimate Relationships)**</u>

When one person evolves, the relationship must recalibrate.

Resist urgency. Don't push them to "be okay" or "move on." Love them in the pause.

Name the shift without blame. Acknowledge that success can change dynamics without being a threat.

Stay curious, not corrective. Ask what they're learning about themselves rather than what's next.

Hold space for grief and pride simultaneously. They may mourn what was lost even as they celebrate what was earned.

Reaffirm belonging. Say, explicitly and often: *"You don't have to perform here."*

<u>**EDUCATION (Students, Graduates, Scholars)**</u>

Achievement doesn't eliminate the need for guidance; it often increases it.

Normalize the anticlimax. Let them know it's common for milestones to feel quiet or hollow.

Shift the question from "What's next?" to "Who are you becoming?"

Help them build new rhythms. Structure disappears after graduation; emotional scaffolding matters.

Avoid comparison stories. Their path doesn't need to mirror yours or anyone else's to be valid.

Celebrate process, not just outcomes. Affirm the discipline, growth, and resilience it took to reach goals and pivot points along the way to larger success.

CAREER (Promotions, Leadership, Entrepreneurship) Elevation often isolates before it empowers.

Acknowledge the loneliness of leadership. Don't romanticize it or dismiss it.

Avoid transactional praise. Recognition should affirm the person, not just their productivity.

Create a confidential space. Leaders need places where they are not "on."

Support reflection before acceleration. New roles deserve intentional onboarding for the self.

Remind them that rest is strategic, not indulgent.

CAREGIVING (Eldercare, Illness, Family Responsibility) Caregiving milestones are rarely celebrated, yet profoundly transformative.

Recognize invisible graduations. Surviving, adapting, and enduring are achievements.

Don't rush gratitude. Caregivers can love deeply and still feel depleted.

Offer specific help, not general concern. Tangible support reduces isolation.

Honor identity beyond the role. They are more than what they provide.

Allow complexity. Relief, sadness, pride, and resentment can coexist.

PARENTING (New phases, Empty Nest, Letting Go)

Every stage of parenting ends with one phase as it begins another.

Name the loss, not just the pride. Let parents grieve the evolution of their parental roles, which can change and even end.

Avoid minimizing statements. Hearing, "You'll get used to it," shuts down processing.

Affirm unseen labor. Parenting success often feels loneliest at transition points.

Encourage reconnection to self. Identity doesn't disappear when a role shifts.

Honor the pause. Becoming a different kind of parent takes time.

A Final Reminder for Supporters

You don't need to fix a lonely graduation.

You need to **witness it**.

Presence is the intervention.
Patience is a gift.
Stillness is the support.

JOURNAL PROMPTS FOR DEEPER REFLECTION ON *LONELY GRADUATION*

Describe a time when you reached a long-awaited goal but felt emotionally unprepared for what followed. What surprised you most about that moment?

What unspoken sacrifices have you made in the pursuit of excellence, and how do they show up in your body or relationships today?

Write a letter to your past self on the night before a major life transition. What truths or cautions would you offer?

When has stillness felt like discomfort rather than peace? What might that tell you about your relationship with productivity and rest?

How do you distinguish between being *alone* and being *lonely*? Where do you feel that difference most intensely?

What does "graduating" from an identity, role, or relationship look like in your current season of life? What emotional weight does that carry?

How has leadership, formal or informal, altered your sense of community or visibility?

What's a "hidden curriculum" you've had to teach yourself? How has that shaped your self-perception?

If you stripped away all titles, accomplishments, and degrees, what would remain as your truest self-definition?

____

____

____

____

____

____

____

____

____

____

____

____

____

____

____

____

Describe a moment when you felt like "the only one" in a room. What did you learn about resilience or self-trust from that experience?

What patterns of external validation do you notice in your life? What would it mean to release them?

Reflect on a time you mentored someone. What parts of yourself did you see in them, and how did that influence your own healing or growth?

Think about someone who helped you navigate an emotional transition. What qualities did they embody that made you feel seen?

134

When have you unintentionally hoarded knowledge or wisdom? What's held you back from sharing these gems more freely?

What story do you think others tell about your success, and what story would *you* rather they knew?

Where in your life do you feel like you're "walking into the next phase"? What mindset or tools do you want to carry with you?

What does communal success mean to you? How can you participate in it more fully?

What new definition of success are you crafting now, and how does it honor both your past and your becoming?

LONELY GRADUATION
REFERENCES

Botha, F., & Bower, M. (2024). Predictors of male loneliness across life stages: An Australian study of longitudinal data. *BMC Public Health*, *24*(1), 1–11. Academic Search Premier.

Bruss, K. V., Seth, P., & Guixiang Zhao. (2024). Loneliness, Lack of Social and Emotional Support, and Mental Health Issues—United States, 2022. *MMWR: Morbidity & Mortality Weekly Report*, *73*(24), 539–545. Academic Search Premier.

Calderon Leon, M. D., Guassi Moreira, J. F., Saragosa-Harris, N. M., Waizman, Y. H., Sedykin, A., Peris, T. S., & Silvers, J. A. (2024). Parent and Friend Relationship Quality and Links to Trajectories of Loneliness During the First Year of College. *Child Psychiatry & Human Development*, *55*(3), 680–694. Academic Search Premier.

Chhajer, R., Chaudhry, S., & Mishra, A. (2024). Combating the mental health challenge of loneliness among urban youth: Could finding meaning in life and experiencing thriving enhance their well-being? *BMC Public Health*, *24*(1), 1–14. Academic Search Premier.

Dor-Haim, P. (2023). Expressions of loneliness: Different perspectives of loneliness among school deputy principals. *Educational Management Administration & Leadership*, *51*(5), 1181–1199. Academic Search Premier.

Jin, J., & Ikeda, H. (2024). The Role of Empathic Communication in the Relationship between Servant Leadership and Workplace Loneliness: A Serial Mediation Model. *Behavioral Sciences (2076-328X)*, *14*(1), 4. Academic Search Premier.

NICHOLS, J., & MCBRIDE, J. (2017). PROMOTED FROM WITHIN: PREPARING BEGINNING EDUCATIONAL LEADERS FOR EXECUTIVE LONELINESS THAT OCCURS IN THEIR NEW POSITION. *College Student Journal*, *51*(1), 47–56. Academic Search Premier.

Nie, Q., Chen, X., & Yu, G. (2023). Linking workplace loneliness to workplace territoriality: A self-protection perspective. *International Journal of Conflict Management (Emerald)*, *34*(2), 299–316. Academic Search Premier.

Pang, N. T. P. (2022). The Tempest: A Reflection on Pandemic Loneliness. *Archives of Psychiatry Research*, *58*(2), 293–296. Academic Search Premier.

Patel, T. A., Stentz, L. A., & Cougle, J. R. (2024). A Multi-Method Analysis of the Role of Social Safety Behavior in Loneliness. *Cognitive Therapy & Research*, *48*(3), 1–12. Academic Search Premier.

Pavlova, T., & Bannikov, G. (2015). Loneliness and Hopelessness in Teenagers. *European Psychiatry*, *30*, 1796–1796. Academic Search Premier.

Sease, T. B., Sandoz, E. K., Yoke, L., Swets, J. A., & Cox, C. R. (2024). Loneliness and Relationship Well-Being: Investigating the Mediating Roles of Relationship Awareness and Distraction among Romantic Partners. *Behavioral Sciences (2076-328X)*, *14*(6), 439. Academic Search Premier.

Stocker, C. M., Gilligan, M., Klopack, E. T., Conger, K. J., Lanthier, R. P., Neppl, T. K., O'Neal, C. W., & Wickrama, K. A. S. (2020). Sibling relationships in older adulthood: Links with loneliness and well-being. *Journal of Family Psychology*, *34*(2), 175–185. Academic Search Premier.

The Ups and Downs of Graduation—Counseling & Psychological Services | Montana State University. (n.d.). Retrieved January 26, 2025, from

https://www.montana.edu/counseling/selfhelp/graduation.ht
ml

Wang, X., Cao, X., Yu, J., Jin, S., Li, S., Chen, L., Liu, Z., Ge, X., & Lu, Y. (2024). Associations of perceived stress with loneliness and depressive symptoms: The mediating role of sleep quality. *BMC Psychiatry*, *24*(1), 1–10. Academic Search Premier.

Wang, Y., & Zeng, Y. (2024). Relationship between loneliness and internet addiction: A meta-analysis. *BMC Public Health*, *24*(1), 1–14. Academic Search Premier.

Yosso, T. J. (2005). Whose culture has capital? A critical race theory discussion of community cultural wealth. *Race Ethnicity and Education*, *8*(1), 69–91. https://doi.org/10.1080/1361332052000341006

Yang, H., Lin, Z., Chen, X., & Peng, J. (2023). Workplace loneliness, ego depletion, and cyberloafing: Can leader problem-focused interpersonal emotion management help? *Internet Research*, *33*(4), 1473–1494. Academic Search Premier

INDEX OF QUOTES